MW01200381

R. CRUMB

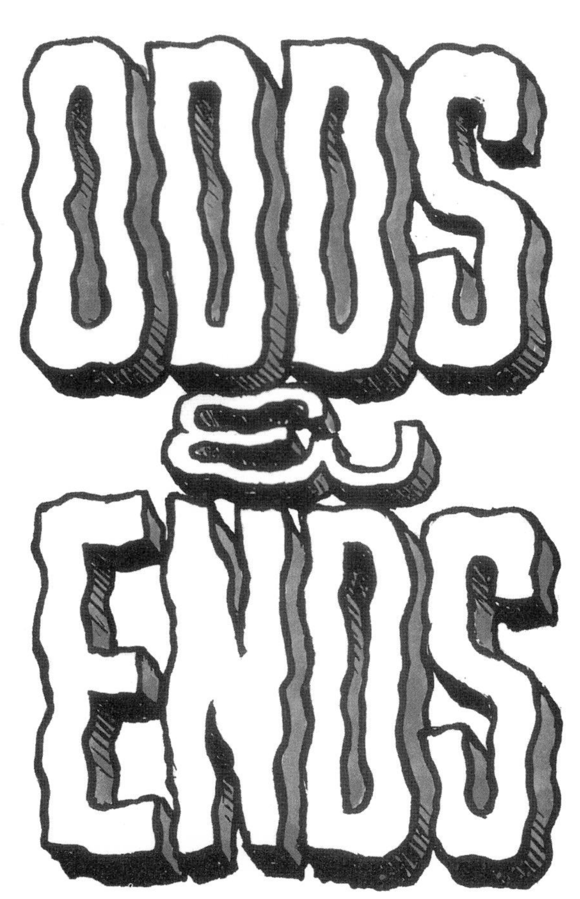

BLOOMSBURY

R. Crumb, *Odds & Ends*,
a chronologically ordered collection
of rare works by Robert Crumb,
with an introduction by Jean-Pierre Mercier.

The publisher would like to thank R. Crumb for allowing access to his archives and providing additional information. Thanks also to the many friends who contributed documents, information and help: Aline Kominsky Crumb, Sophie Crumb, Lora Fountain, Denis Kitchen, Richard Kuiters, Eric Gilbert and Jean-Pierre Mercier

Private eye: Hansje Joustra
Book design: Joost Swarte
Layout: Marc Nagtzaam
Text editing, production:
Mat Schifferstein

Document photography: Degens repro, Haarlem
Lithography: De Lithografen uit Haarlem, Velserbroek
Typesetting: Nico Swanink, Haarlem
Printing: LenoirSchuringSpelthuis, Amstelveen
Binding: Stokkink, Amsterdam

First published by Oog & Blik, Nieuwe Hemweg 7e-7f,
1013 BG Amsterdam, The Netherlands

Published in Great Britain and the USA 2001 by
Bloomsbury Publishing Plc, New York and London

Bloomsbury Publishing Plc, 38 Soho Square, London W1V 5DF

Distributed to the trade in the USA by St. Martin's Press

A CIP catalogue record is available from the British Library
A CIP catalogue record is available from the Library of Congress

UK ISBN 0 7475 5309 2
USA ISBN 1-58234-136-2

First U.S. Edition 2001
10 9 8 7 6 5 4 3 2 1

On the frontcover:
Selfportrait by R. Crumb,
Paris 1990–2000

On the backcover:
Advertisement for
Pepper & Stern Rare Books,
Inc., Los Angeles, 1987
Drawing for the cover of
Snatch Comics,
San Francisco, 1969

INTRODUCTION
by Jean-Pierre Mercier

Who is Robert Crumb? “Mr. Sixties”, the godfather of the underground comic or the loudmouth of the eighties? A character nostalgic of pre industrial America or just another sex maniac?

The question may seem irrelevant to all those who rightly prefer the works to the artists. In the case of Crumb, however, it may be a legitimate question as he puts so much of himself into his creations. In “The many faces of Robert Crumb”, published in 1972, he seemed to anticipate his eventual fame and reacted to it in a quite peculiar way, dazzling the reader with an overdose of irony and ambiguity.

And now, almost thirty years later, we can add new experiences to the list: a wise man drawn by mysticism, an American in exile (torn from his country), a grapho-maniac who has dedicated his life to his drawings...

However, there is a less apparent characterization of Crumb that does more justice to the artist: Crumb, the medieval man. Crumb has a passion for medieval art and for the artists whose work has survived the test of time: Jeroen Bosch, Breughel-the-Elder. He has found inspiration in their paintings and engravings, he identifies with their humour, their gloom and their power of expression. At the same time, one can imagine that he also longs for an age when artists were considered craftsmen who concentrated on their art and developed a personal style without being restricted by a central authority. There is no question that religion was powerful, but it did not prevent these strong personalities to

The Silly Pigeons
made for Help, 1965

The Foot Massage
for Tom Marion, 1986

express plainly and without pretence the world they knew, as well as their intimate hopes and dreams. Artists conscious of their value to society produced their paintings like a cabinet-maker made furniture: with a technique based on a long line of experience, that they should please and serve without ever losing sight of their own personality.

One can easily imagine Robert Crumb in the back of a studio situated in the centre of an old town, working non-stop to satisfy the needs of a small but loyal reading public, alternating engravings, paintings, sign-boards and illuminated designs.

Indeed, what else has he been doing for the past three decades, bent over his drawing board? Working non-stop, producing comic books, record covers and illustrations, much to the pleasure of his fans all over the world.

During the last ten years or so, publishers from both sides of the Atlantic have been working on publishing the complete works of Robert Crumb, including all the comic books and sketch-books that Crumb has been drawing since the early sixties. In doing so they have made available an enormous amount of his art work that had been published in hundreds of cheap comic magazines and a variety of small press publications.
In 1995, Oog en Blik took the next step by compiling more marginal products of his graphic oeuvre: a collection of drawings Crumb made on paper napkins in

Buttons for Kitchen
Sink Press, 1977, 1983

Gina in Hell, 1988

Portrait of Frank Zappa for The New Yorker. 1992

restaurants while waiting to be served.

Now, in this all-new collection you'll find another number of products which represent a rather unknown side of Robert Crumb: Crumb the "commercial" artist. This book contains a variety of drawings Crumb made for friends and relatives: birth announcements, wedding invitations, birthday cards, invitations, business cards and advertisements...

If you're a Crumb-addict, no further description is necessary. You will enjoy this book to the fullest, especially since the greater part of its content is quite unknown. If you've just discovered the artist, this book is as good an entrance to his universe as any other. In these drawings, commissioned throughout a period of more than 30 years, it is easy to recognize the hand of Crumb. He has created these drawings with the same tenderloving care he uses for everything he does. A touch of irony is never far away, and even if some of the drawings are rather light-hearted, you will immediately notice that Crumb has put his entire soul into every single picture he has made. He has never done otherwise.

Jean-Pierre Mercier is staff-member of the CNBDI, the comic strip museum in Angoulême, France, and a personal friend of Robert Crumb.

A PUBLISHERS NOTE

Most of Robert Crumb's art work has been made available to his fans. It has been published in books and magazines, and even his sketchbooks are published in their entirety.

But with Crumb, there's always more. He does work for marginal magazines like 'Winds of Change', and then, all of a sudden, he shows up in 'The New Yorker'. He draws birth announcements, portraits or publicity posters for friends, neighbours and relatives.

His work can be found all over the world – which makes it hard to trace, but, thanks to Crumb's own collection, we are able to show a substantial part of it in 'Odds & Ends'.

The drawings are arranged chronologically. At the top of the page, you will see the year of appearance of the drawings presented. For any exceptions, the correct year of publication is mentioned in the legend. When Robert Crumb has given us background details, we share these with the reader.

Left-centred text refers to the drawings on the left-hand page; right-centred text refers to the drawings on the right-hand page.

WHAT WOULD YOU LIKE TO KNOW?

Card, cover drawing and inside text, unpublished.
1963

Valentine card, cover drawing and inside text, unpublished.
1963

Ecolian Election Number, drawing for a high school newspaper. Dover, Delaware.

Merry Christmas card, made after working hours at American Greetings, unpublished.
1963

The Crucifiction and Death of Puff the Magic Dragon, a 'sarcastic' gift for a girl who loved the song Puff the Magic Dragon. When she saw it, she cried and did not want it. Unpublished.
1963

1964

CRUMB

From a booklet called For You With Love, pages 22 & 23. Lingham & Yoni Ltd.

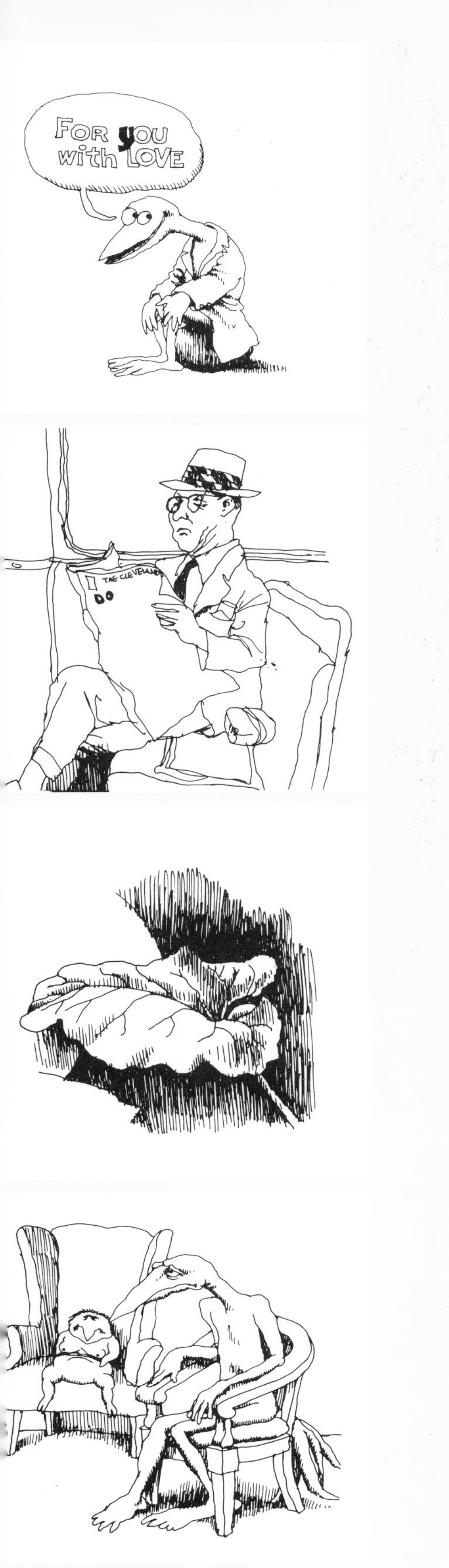

lingham & yoni, ltd.
yellow springs, ohio
© 1964

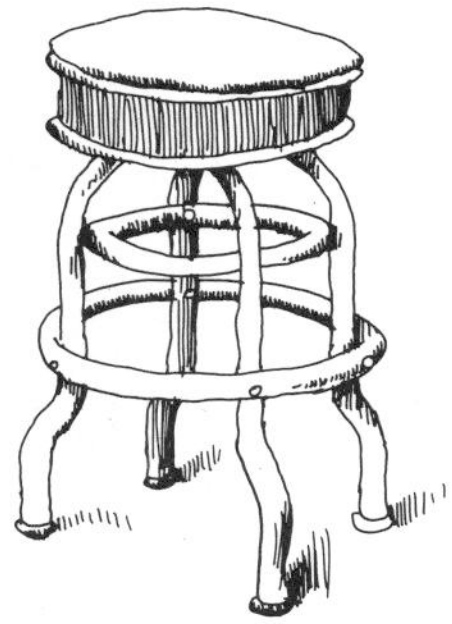

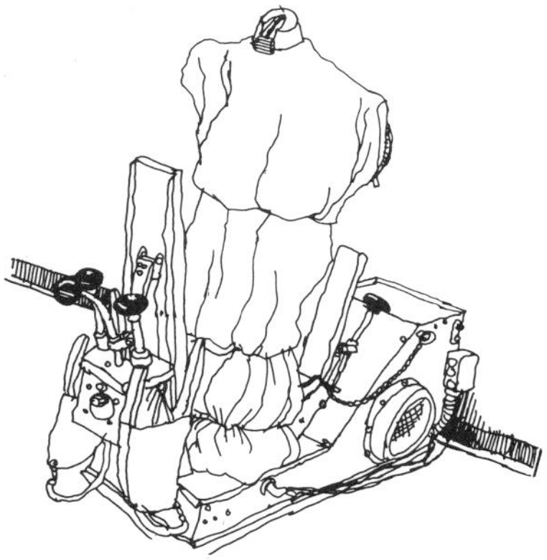

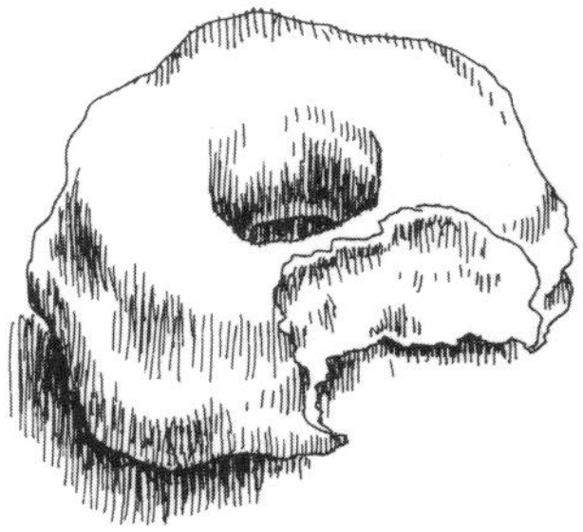

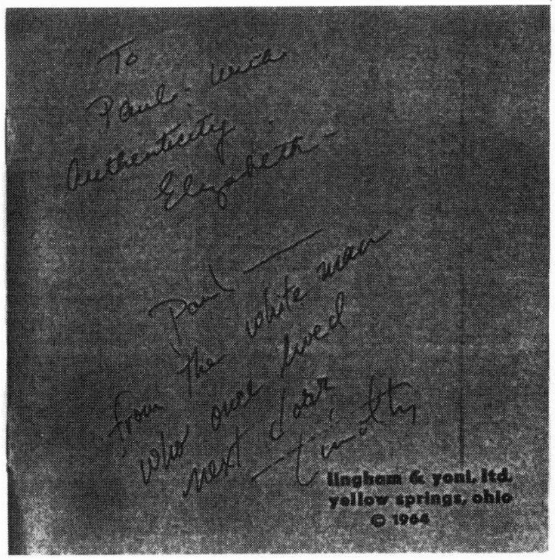

i made a special trip down town to get you this Birthday card at exactly 8:30 Monday morning.....that's when they change the clothes on the mannequins.

Happy Birthday

Happy Birthday (idea by John Gibbons), a greeting card 'tested' by Walgreen Drugstores: the wife of the owner of the Walgreen chain considered this card objectionable, obscene and perverse. Consequently it was withdrawn from distribution. Published by American Greetings, Cleveland.

Double birthday card with panels, American Greetings, Cleveland.

They've got
His and Hers Bath Towels...

....His and Hers Pajamas...

....His and Hers Beds...

....so, in keeping with the trend.....

....His and Hers Anniversary Cards!

Congratulations

....His and Hers Anniversary Cards!

Happy Anniversary To You!

Happy Anniversary to you too!

Congratulations

Birthday card. American Greetings, Cleveland.

There are a lot of things worse than having another Birthday. What would you do if you were in Jack's place? What would you do if you were in Mary's place?

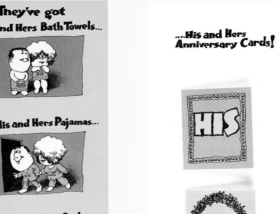

....I THOUGHT SO!!!
Oh Well, Happy Birthday Anyway

I Thought So, birthday card, American Greetings, Cleveland.

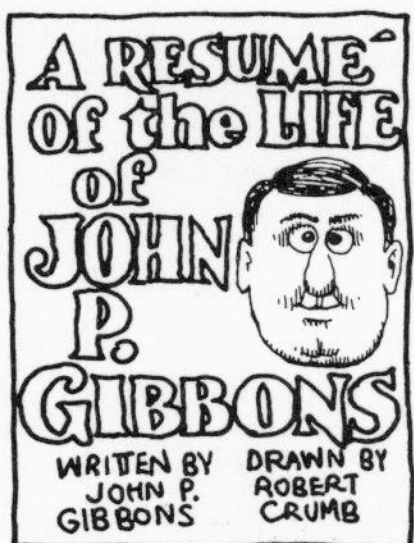
A RESUME' of the LIFE of JOHN P. GIBBONS
WRITEN BY JOHN P. GIBBONS
DRAWN BY ROBERT CRUMB

BORN SEPTEMBER 2, 1933
HA HA
DELIVERY ROOM
HAW HAW

EDUCATION: ATTENDED ST. JEROME'S GRADE SCHOOL IN CLEVELAND.

ATTENDED CATHEDRAL LATIN HIGH SCHOOL FOR ONE YEAR....
CATHEDRAL LATIN

ATTENDED ST. IGNATIUS HIGH SCHOOL FOR ONE YEAR....
ST. IGNATIUS

ATTENDED COLLINWOOD HIGH FOR ONE YEAR...
COLLINWOOD HIGH SCHOOL

AND FINALLY GRADUATED FROM WITHROW HIGH SCHOOL IN CINCINNATI...

WITHROW HIGH SCHOOL

COLLEGE: BUTLER UNIVERSITY, INDIANAPOLIS, INDIANA...

MILITARY SERVICE: ENTERED U.S. ARMY IN 1956...
LOOK, JOHN! HERE COME SOME OF YOUR ARMY BUDDIES!
MP
MP

COMBAT EXPERIENCE: COLUMBUS, GEORGIA
DAYUM NO' THUN SCUM!
GIT OUTA THIS TOWN!
YANKEES!

RECIEVED HONORABLE DISCHARGE AND SERVED SIX YEARS IN RESERVES...
BROWMM BWOM!
POW! POW!

BUSINESS EXPERIENCE: AFTER WORKING FOR A NUMBER OF COMMERCIAL RADIO STATIONS AS ANNOUNCER, WRITER, ENGINEER, ETC, ETC....
WHIC RADIO

I DECIDED TO BECOME STRICTLY A WRITER...
BAGGAGE

...AND FINALLY FOUND MYSELF IN THE HI-BROW STUDIO OF AMERICAN GREETINGS CORPORATION...
HI BROW STUDIO

...A NEWLY FORMED GROUP OF WRITERS AND ARTISTS...

DEVOTED TO BRINGING FRESH, ORIGINAL AND TRULY FUNNY MATERIAL TO THE GREETING CARD BUSINESS...
FINISHED CARDS
FINISHED CARDS
10,000 JOKES

...AFTER SIX YEARS, I HAVE DONE ALL I CAN FOR THE STUDIO,...IT MUST NOW STAND OR FALL ON IT'S OWN MERITS...

TRY AS THEY MAY, THE COMPANY OFFICIALS CANNOT PERSUADE ME TO STAY...
PRIVATE OFFICE OF J. P. GIBBONS

EVEN HUGE RAISES IN PAY CANNOT DISSUADE ME FROM MY DECISION TO LEAVE AMERICAN GREETINGS...

I AM VERY INTERESTED IN WORKING FOR YOU, BUT MUST WARN YOU THAT I AM BEING CONSIDERED FOR A BIG RAILROAD JOB...
DELANCEY

...A KEY POST IN ONE OF THE LARGER ADVERTISING AGENCIES....
CLABBER GIRL BAKING POWDER

... A POSITION WITH A MAJOR AIRLINE...

...A TOP-FLIGHT JOB IN COMMUNICATIONS....
WESTERN UNION

...AND AN EXECUTIVE OPENING IN A FAST-RISING YOUNG ORGANIZATION.

I'LL HOLD THEM OFF AS LONG AS I CAN, PENDING HEARING FROM YOU...
ACME COLLECTION AGENCY
PEERLESS BILL COLLECTORS

apt. 4
IS COMING

A Resumé of the Life of John P. Gibbons, unpublished comic, pages 1, 2 & 3.
1964

Apt. 4 Is Coming, portrait of Liz Johnston on a card, Cleveland, published by Apt. 4.
1964

I'd Like to Give You a Big Squeeze, Topps Monster Gum card, Topps, New York.

Reverse side of Topps Monster Gum card, Topps, New York.

You Have a Peach of a Complexion, Topps Monster Gum card, Topps, New York.

Hairy!, reverse side of Topps Monster Gum card, Topps, New York.

You Have the Skin I Love to Touch, Topps Monster Gum card, Topps, New York.

And Clutch!, reverse side of Topps Monster Gum card, Topps, New York.

Decomposition, illustration for East Village Other.

I'd like to give you a BIG SQUEEZE
over...
27
You have a PEACH of a complexion
OVER
HAIRY!
5
YOU HAVE THE SKIN I LOVE TO TOUCH
TURN OVER
16
Robt. Crumb –

THE HEAP YEARS of the Auto~1946~59

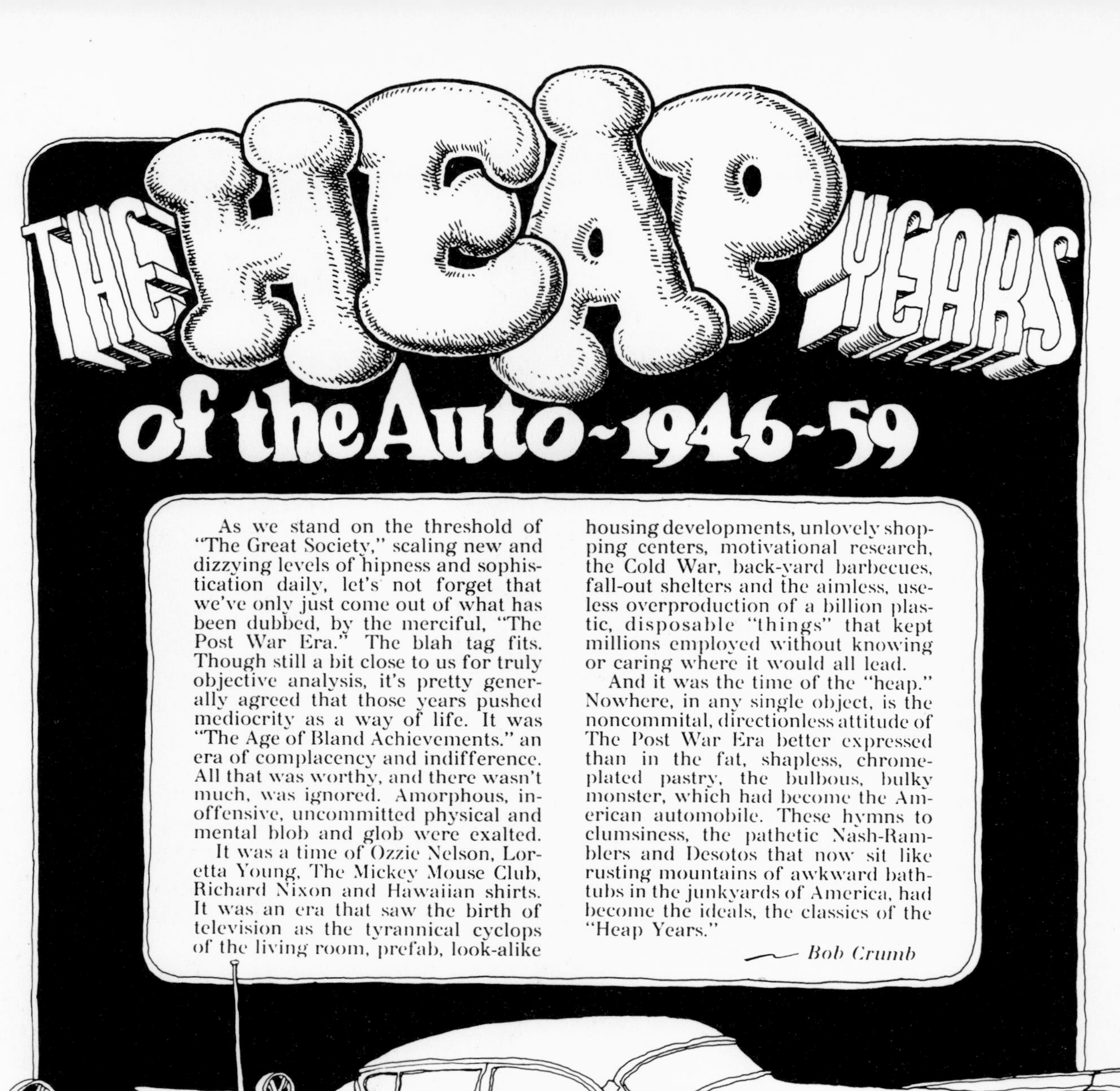

As we stand on the threshold of "The Great Society," scaling new and dizzying levels of hipness and sophistication daily, let's not forget that we've only just come out of what has been dubbed, by the merciful, "The Post War Era." The blah tag fits. Though still a bit close to us for truly objective analysis, it's pretty generally agreed that those years pushed mediocrity as a way of life. It was "The Age of Bland Achievements," an era of complacency and indifference. All that was worthy, and there wasn't much, was ignored. Amorphous, inoffensive, uncommitted physical and mental blob and glob were exalted.

It was a time of Ozzie Nelson, Loretta Young, The Mickey Mouse Club, Richard Nixon and Hawaiian shirts. It was an era that saw the birth of television as the tyrannical cyclops of the living room, prefab, look-alike housing developments, unlovely shopping centers, motivational research, the Cold War, back-yard barbecues, fall-out shelters and the aimless, useless overproduction of a billion plastic, disposable "things" that kept millions employed without knowing or caring where it would all lead.

And it was the time of the "heap." Nowhere, in any single object, is the noncommital, directionless attitude of The Post War Era better expressed than in the fat, shapless, chrome-plated pastry, the bulbous, bulky monster, which had become the American automobile. These hymns to clumsiness, the pathetic Nash-Ramblers and Desotos that now sit like rusting mountains of awkward bathtubs in the junkyards of America, had become the ideals, the classics of the "Heap Years."

— *Bob Crumb*

1958 Buick

R. Crumb

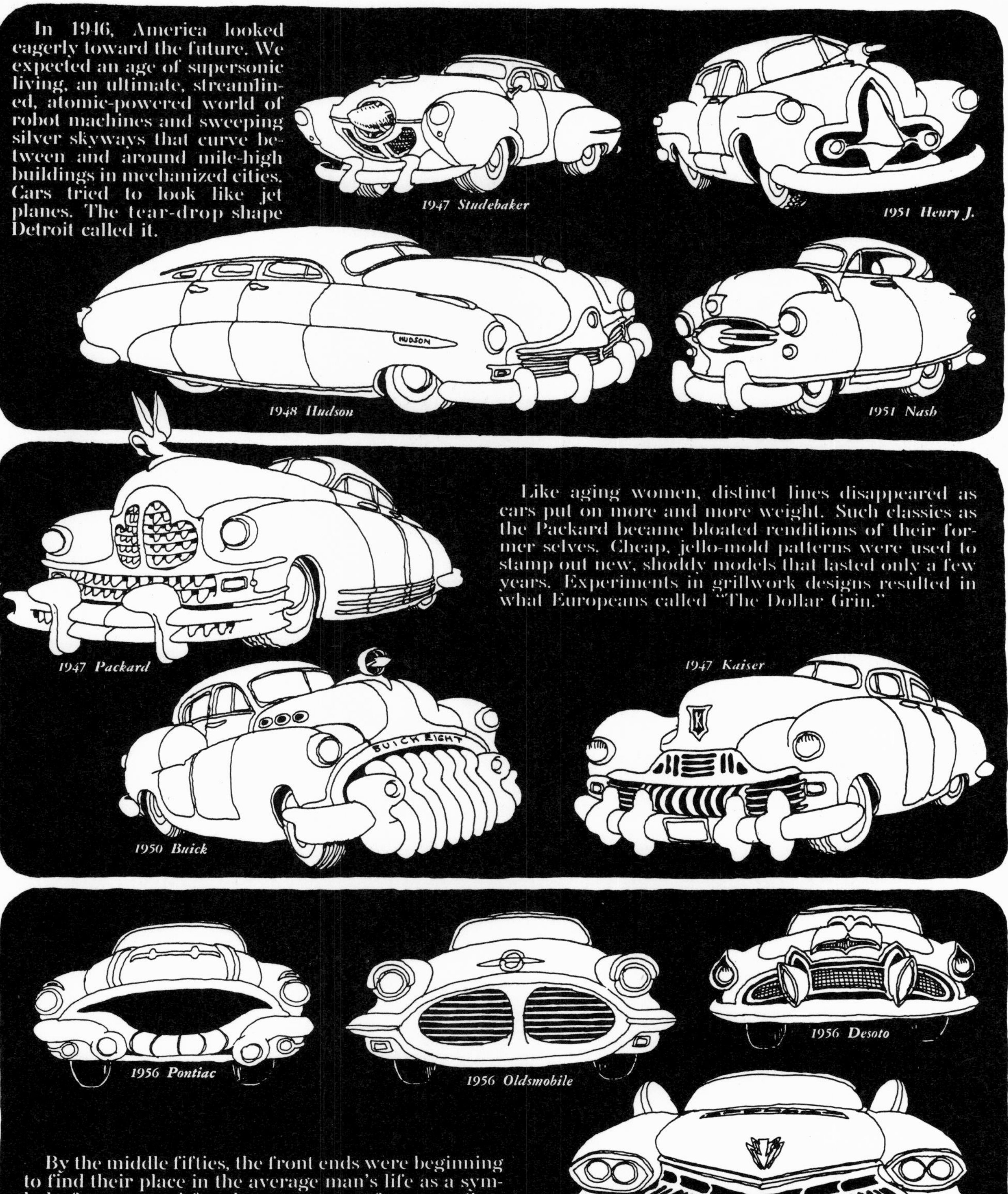

In 1946, America looked eagerly toward the future. We expected an age of supersonic living, an ultimate, streamlined, atomic-powered world of robot machines and sweeping silver skyways that curve between and around mile-high buildings in mechanized cities. Cars tried to look like jet planes. The tear-drop shape Detroit called it.

1947 Studebaker · *1951 Henry J.* · *1948 Hudson* · *1951 Nash*

Like aging women, distinct lines disappeared as cars put on more and more weight. Such classics as the Packard became bloated renditions of their former selves. Cheap, jello-mold patterns were used to stamp out new, shoddy models that lasted only a few years. Experiments in grillwork designs resulted in what Europeans called "The Dollar Grin."

1947 Packard · *1947 Kaiser* · *1950 Buick*

1956 Pontiac · *1956 Oldsmobile* · *1956 Desoto*

By the middle fifties, the front ends were beginning to find their place in the average man's life as a symbol of power and freedom, a means of escape. Cars began to look tough, mean, belligerent. Horsepower was the magic word, and cars started sporting fancy names like "Fury," "Hornet," "Golden Hawk," "Thunderbird," "Firebird," "Thundercloud," etc.

1958 Dodge

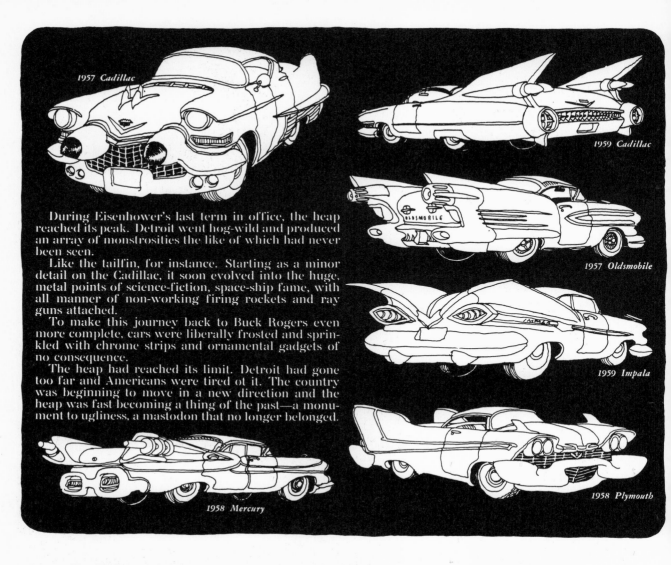

1957 Cadillac

1959 Cadillac

During Eisenhower's last term in office, the heap reached its peak. Detroit went hog-wild and produced an array of monstrosities the like of which had never been seen.

Like the tailfin, for instance. Starting as a minor detail on the Cadillac, it soon evolved into the huge, metal points of science-fiction, space-ship fame, with all manner of non-working firing rockets and ray guns attached.

To make this journey back to Buck Rogers even more complete, cars were liberally frosted and sprinkled with chrome strips and ornamental gadgets of no consequence.

The heap had reached its limit. Detroit had gone too far and Americans were tired of it. The country was beginning to move in a new direction and the heap was fast becoming a thing of the past—a monument to ugliness, a mastodon that no longer belonged.

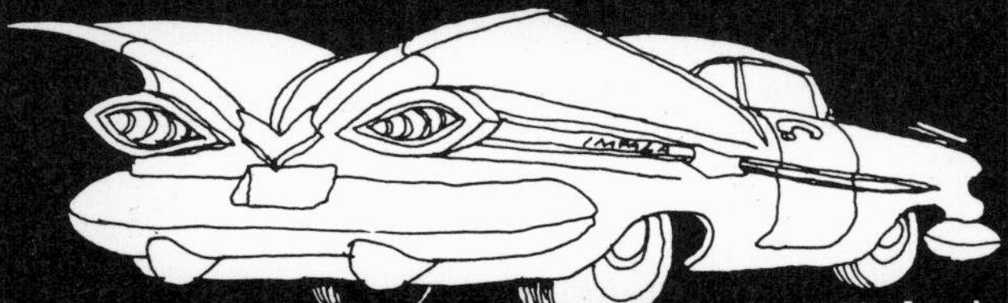

1957 Oldsmobile

1959 Impala

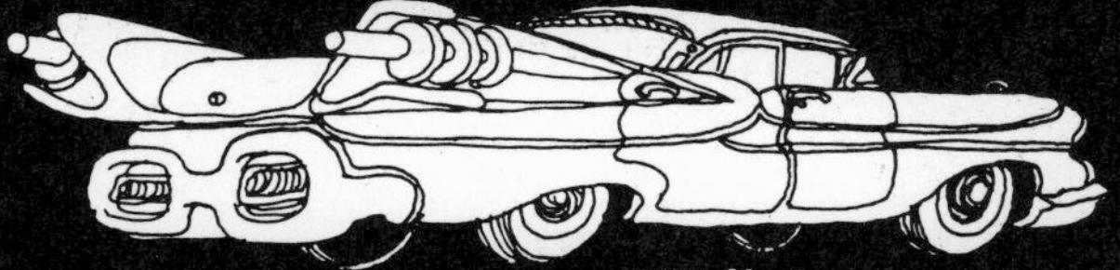

1958 Mercury

1958 Plymouth

One last, desperate fling was made to keep the heap alive, but it was a total disaster, a miserable failure. Nobody was buying heaps anymore. Suddenly, there were all these funny little European cars all over the place, and Detroit saw the light. The "compact" was born. Then came the American sportscar. And now, we've come full cycle, and the big, powerful classic commands the market again.

The heap is dead. They just don't make cars like that anymore, thank whatever-it-is that guides the hand of Detroit and dictates public taste.

The Heap Years of the Auto 1946-1959, three page-article and illustrations.

What's new?

Old-fashioned Bubble Gum

Good old-fashioned bubble gum, a big juicy chunk of it, twist-wrapped the way kids used to love it (and still do!) with a brand new flavor appeal. We call it Topps 1¢ GIANT TWIST WRAPPED BUBBLE GUM. You'll call it a great new seller! Be old-fashioned the modern way. Order today!

BONUS: 79¢ DISPENSER PACK OF SCHICK STAINLESS BLADES FREE PER BOX

EXTRA BONUS: BAZOOKA GIFT CERTIFICATES FREE IN EVERY BOX, TOO, GOOD FOR LUXURY PREMIUMS LIKE G.E. APPLIANCES, CORNING WARE COOKERY, LONGINES WATCHES, AND MANY, MANY MORE VALUABLE GIFTS, FREE.

Topps Giant Bubble Gum, advertisement.

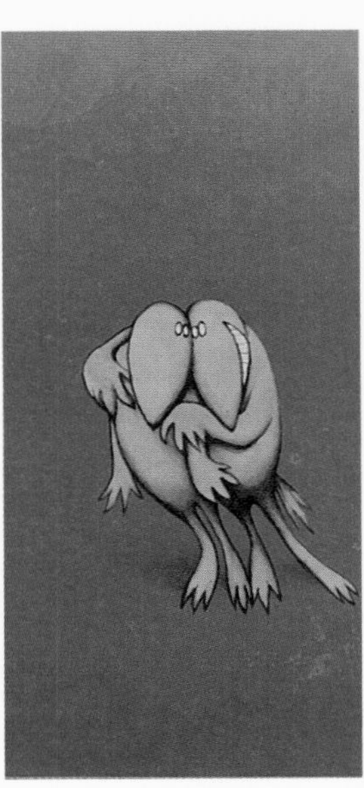

Unpublished greeting card art.

CHEESIS K. REIST in THE DETROIT AVENUE STORY

R. Crumb

Y'KNOW WHAT I NEED? Y'KNOW WHAT I WANT? Y'KNOW WHAT I'M GETTIN'?

SLURP SLURP

WELL IT WON'T BE LONG NOW

HEY THERE MISTER GRILL MAN! GIMME ONE O' THEM DEELISHUS LI'L... SCRUMPSHUS LI'L....

HAMBURGERS

YUM YUM

DROOL

COMIN' RIGHT UP!.. YES SIR!..

CRACKLE POP

HERE Y'ARE, MAN... HOT 'N' HEARTY 'N' PLUMP AS YA PLEASE!

YEAH YEAH!

OH YOU PERTY LITTLE THING... I'M GONNA GIVE YA TH' MUSTARD AN' I'M GONNA GIVE YA KETCHUP!

DILL PICKLE

HO HO! NOW WOULD YOU TAKE A LOOK AT THAT HAMBURGER!

WOT A BEAUTY! WOT A WINNER!

LI'L HAMBURGER, I'M LOOKIN' AT YOU WITH NOTHIN' BUT LOVE, YOU MAY BELIEVE!

AN' IT IS NOT WITH MALICE THAT I TELL YOU, BABY, YOU MUST DIE SO'S THAT I MAY LIVE! YEP!

UH HUH!

LISSEN, PAL, I'LL FILL YOU IN... THAT BURGER KNOWS THE SCORE!

THAT'S RIGHT, BUDDY! DIG' RIGHT IN! THAT'S WHAT IT'S WAITIN' FOR!

ONLY KEEP IN MIND, SIR, WHEN YOU'VE SCARFED ME DOWN...

...THAT'S ONLY HALF OF THE MERRY-GO-ROUND!

I GOTCHA KID! I GOTCHA GOOD I DID!

HAW HAW

CHOFF MUNCH

CHOFF

SLURP

NOW IT'S YOUR TURN! YOUR TURN TO GIVE YOURSELF UP! YOUR TURN TO DIE!

SHADDUP!

CRASH

LEMME OUTA THIS CREEPY JOINT!

HAMBURGER

Unpublished sketch, made in Cleveland. 1965

Advertisement for Nostalgia Illustrated, Nostalgia Press, New York.

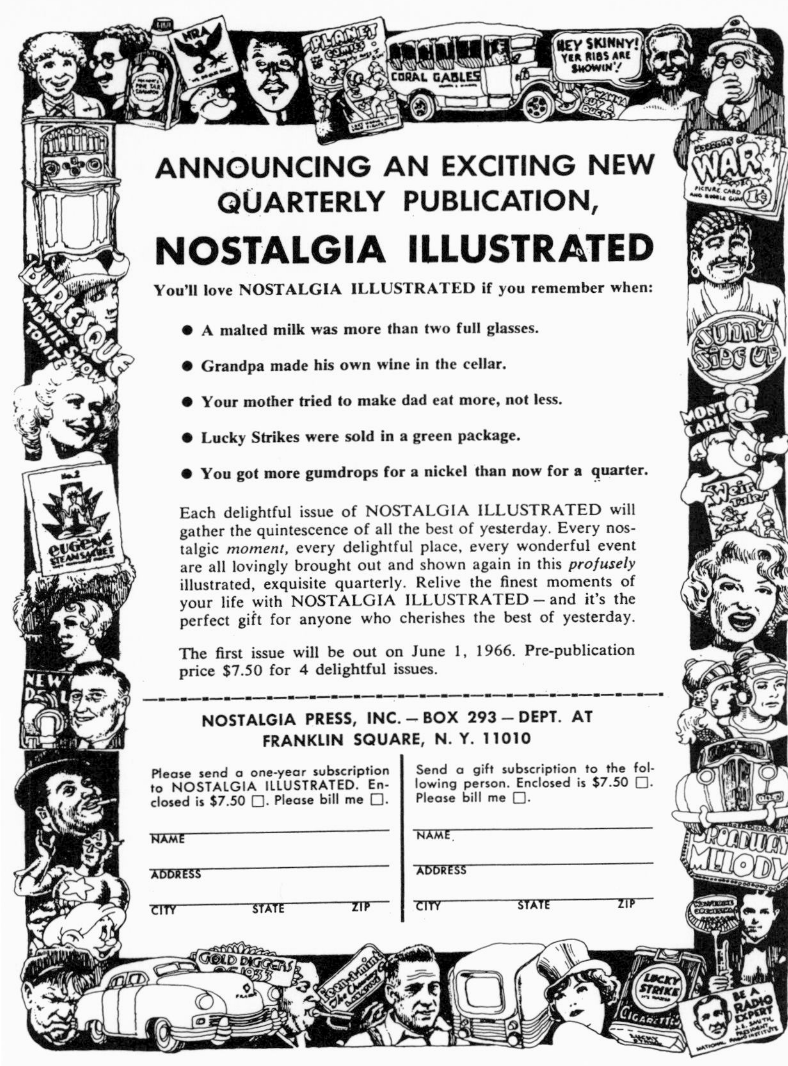

Cheesis K. Reist in the Detroit Avenue Story, comic, pages 1, 2 & 3, published by D.A. Levy, Cleveland.

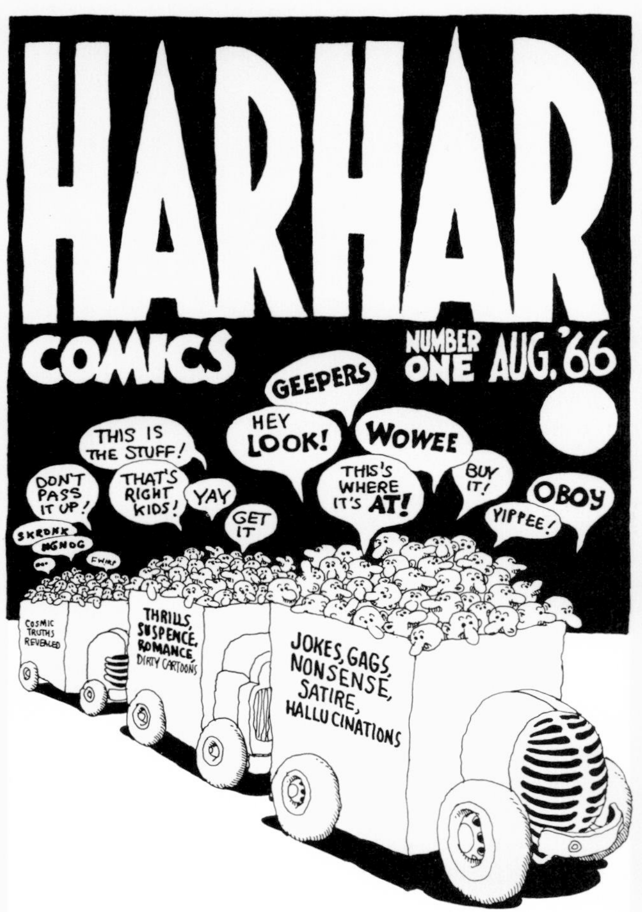
HARHAR
COMICS
NUMBER ONE AUG. '66
GEEPERS
HEY LOOK!
WOWEE
THIS IS THE STUFF!
DON'T PASS IT UP!
THAT'S RIGHT KIDS!
YAY
GET IT
THIS'S WHERE IT'S AT!
BUY IT!
OBOY
YIPPEE!
COSMIC TRUTHS REVEALED
THRILLS, SUSPENCE, ROMANCE, DIRTY CARTOONS
JOKES, GAGS, NONSENSE, SATIRE, HALLUCINATIONS

Girl Walking Away,
watercolor,
publisher unknown.

Cover of
Harhar Comics,
Number One
as published in All Stars,
San Francisco Comic Book.

Cover of Zap Comix,
number 1,
published in All Stars,
San Francisco Comic Book.
1967

It's the Cat's Meow, poster.
1967

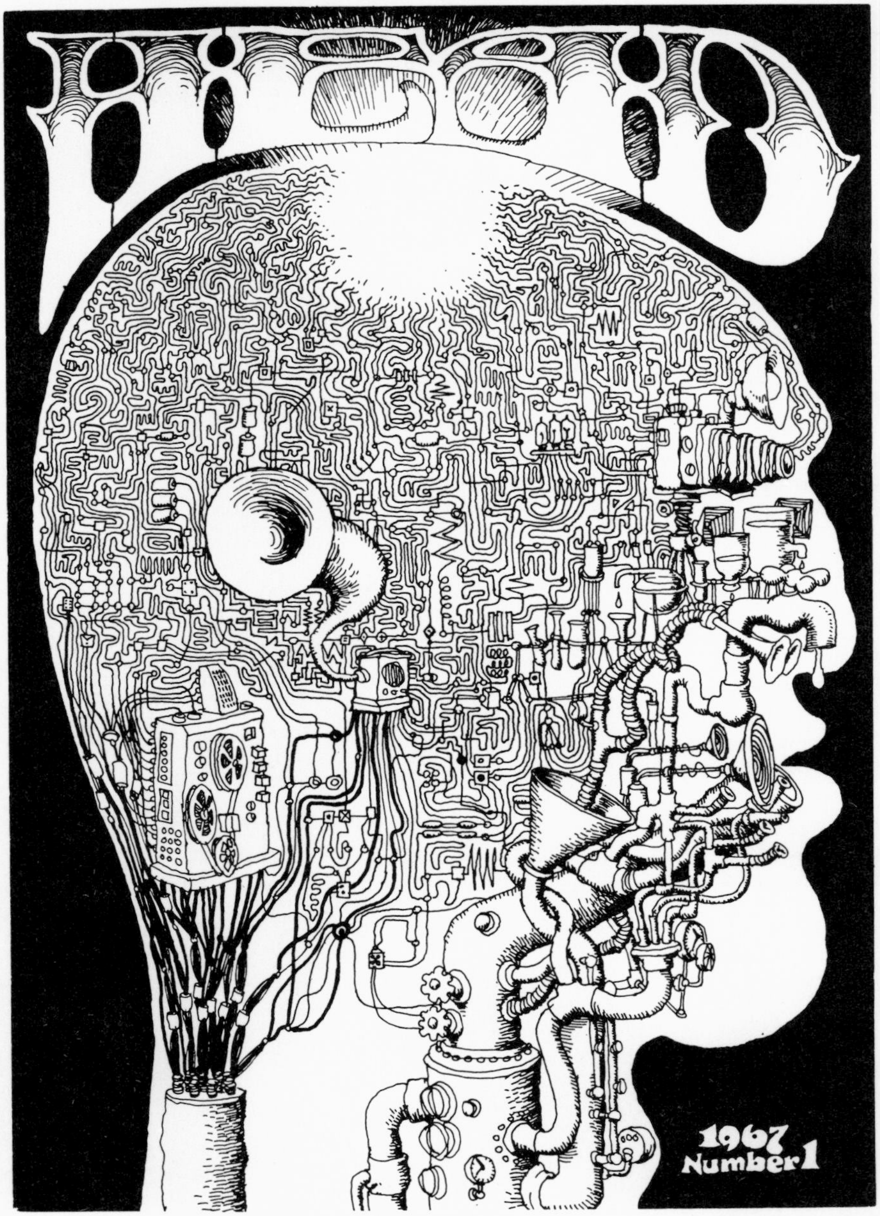

1967 Number 1

Bedrock One, flyer for a festival.

Cover of Head magazine, number 1, published in All Stars, San Francisco Comic Book.

Open Skull Press, letter-head for Doug Blazek, editor of Open Skull Press.

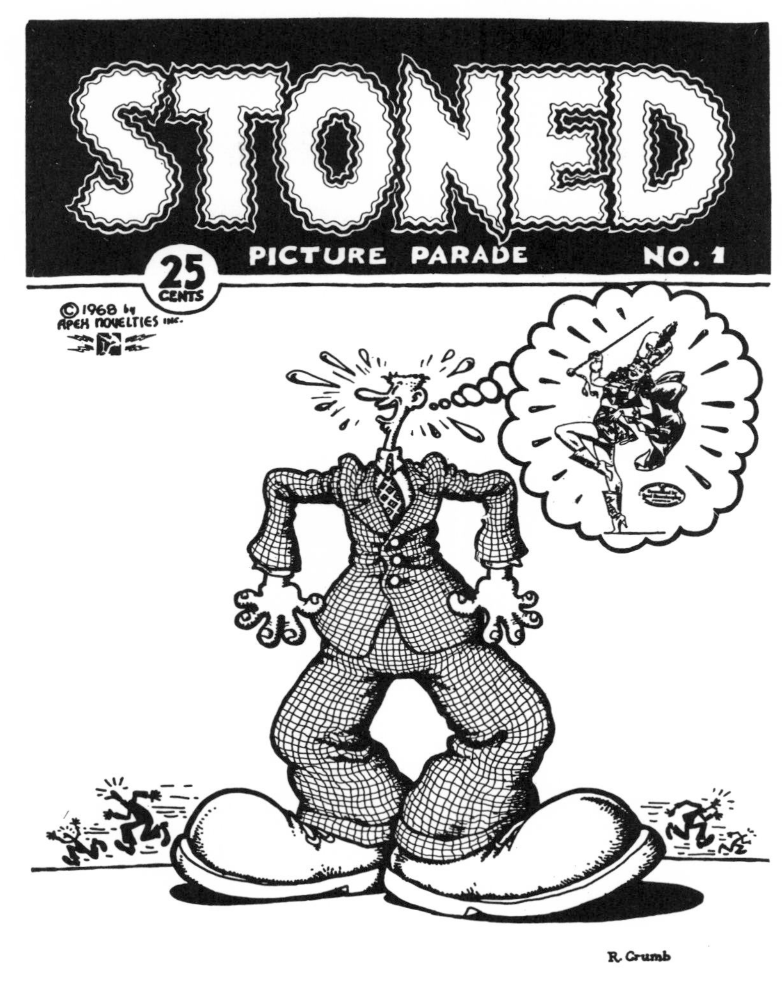

Cover of Stoned magazine, number 1, Apex Novelties, San Francisco 1968

Comic in Stoned magazine, number 1, Apex Novelties, San Francisco. 1968

...but he laid an egg at his first performance!

(happy Easter)

...but I'm not as quick as I used to be!

happy birthday anyway

Birthday card, American Greetings, Cleveland.

Happy Easter, card, American Greetings, Cleveland.

Happy Birthday Anyway, card, American Greetings, Cleveland.

Card, American Greetings, Cleveland.

Happy Birthday, card, American Greetings, Cleveland.

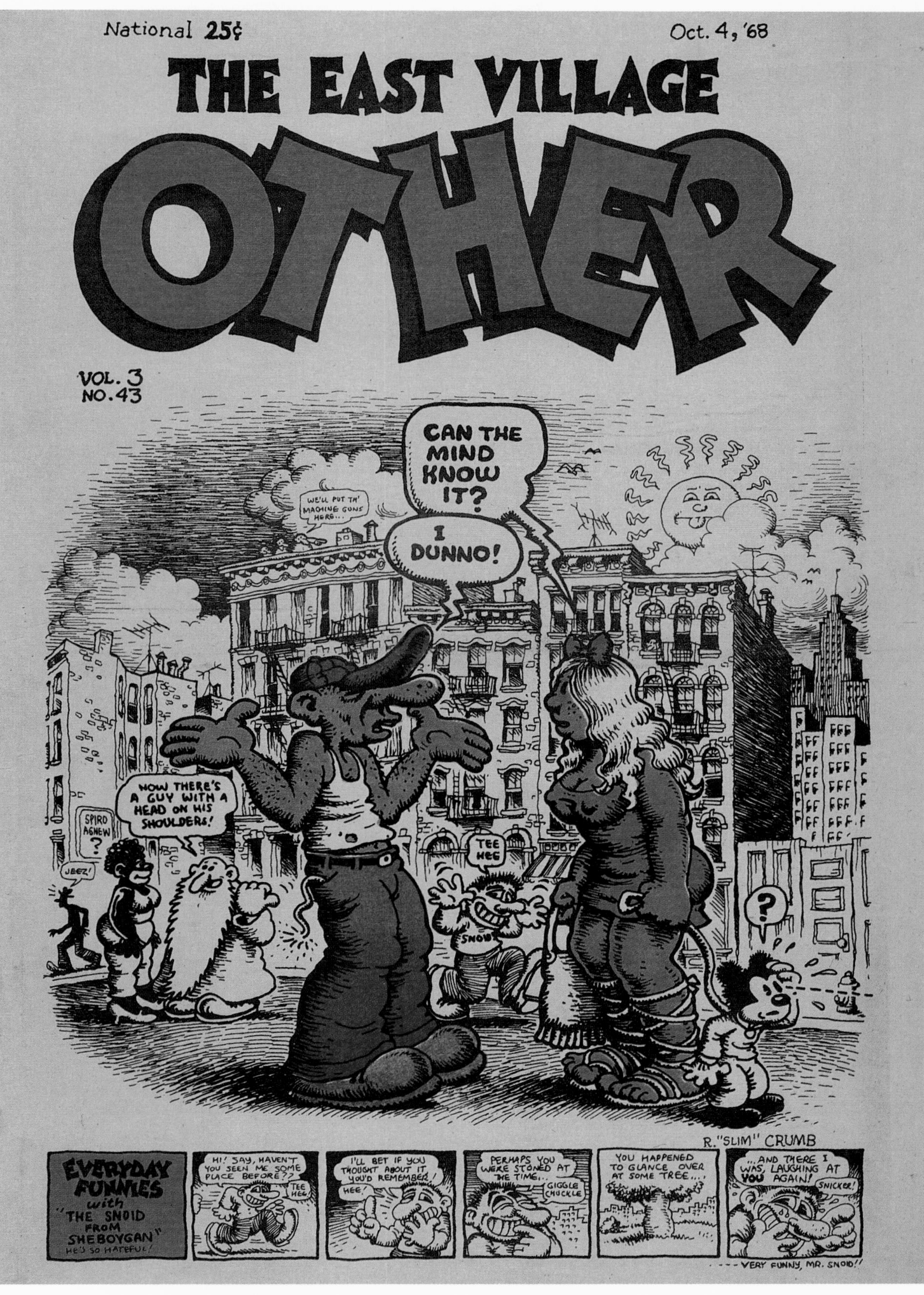

Can the Mind Know It?, cover of The East Village Other, volume 3, number 43. New York.

ARE PEOPLE THINKING MORE AND ENJOYING IT LESS ??

If Ya Can't Say Yep Say Nope, cover of Nope magazine, number 6, published by Jay M. Kinney.

Are People Thinking More and Enjoying It Less?, cover drawing for Nope magazine, number 7, published by Jay M. Kinney.

Kalling All Kool Kustomers, advertisement for Zap Comix in Stoned magazine, number 1, Apex Novelties, San Francisco.

Cover of Zap Comix, number 3, as published in All Stars, San Francisco Comic Books.

Everyday funnies
WHAT TH-
WHAT'S GOING ON HERE?!
???

UHOH!
MOMMY MOMMY

I DON'T GET IT!
HOLY JEEZIZ!

LET'S GIT OUTA HERE!
YOW
EER

HEYWAIDAMININ YA BASTICHIZ!

YER ALL UNNER ARRESTID!
HA HA HAW HA HA HA HA HAW HA

HELICON
SPRING '69
C'MERE KID!
THAT OL' DEVIL MOUNTAIN STILL GRABS 'EM! HEH HEH
HMPH
DIET COLA
R. CRUMB

NO. 2
SNATCH COMICS
69 ISSUE

Helicon
OW!
OY VEY!
LAWN GUYLIN YOONIBURSTITY
SPRING of '69
VOL. 6 NO. 3

Everyday Funnies, comic on back cover of Helicon magazine, spring '69, volume 6, number 3, Lawn Guylin Yooniburstity.

Helicon, cover and title page of this magazine, spring '69, volume 6, number 3, Lawn Guylin Yooniburstity.

Cover of Snatch Comics, as published in All Stars, San Francisco Comic Books.

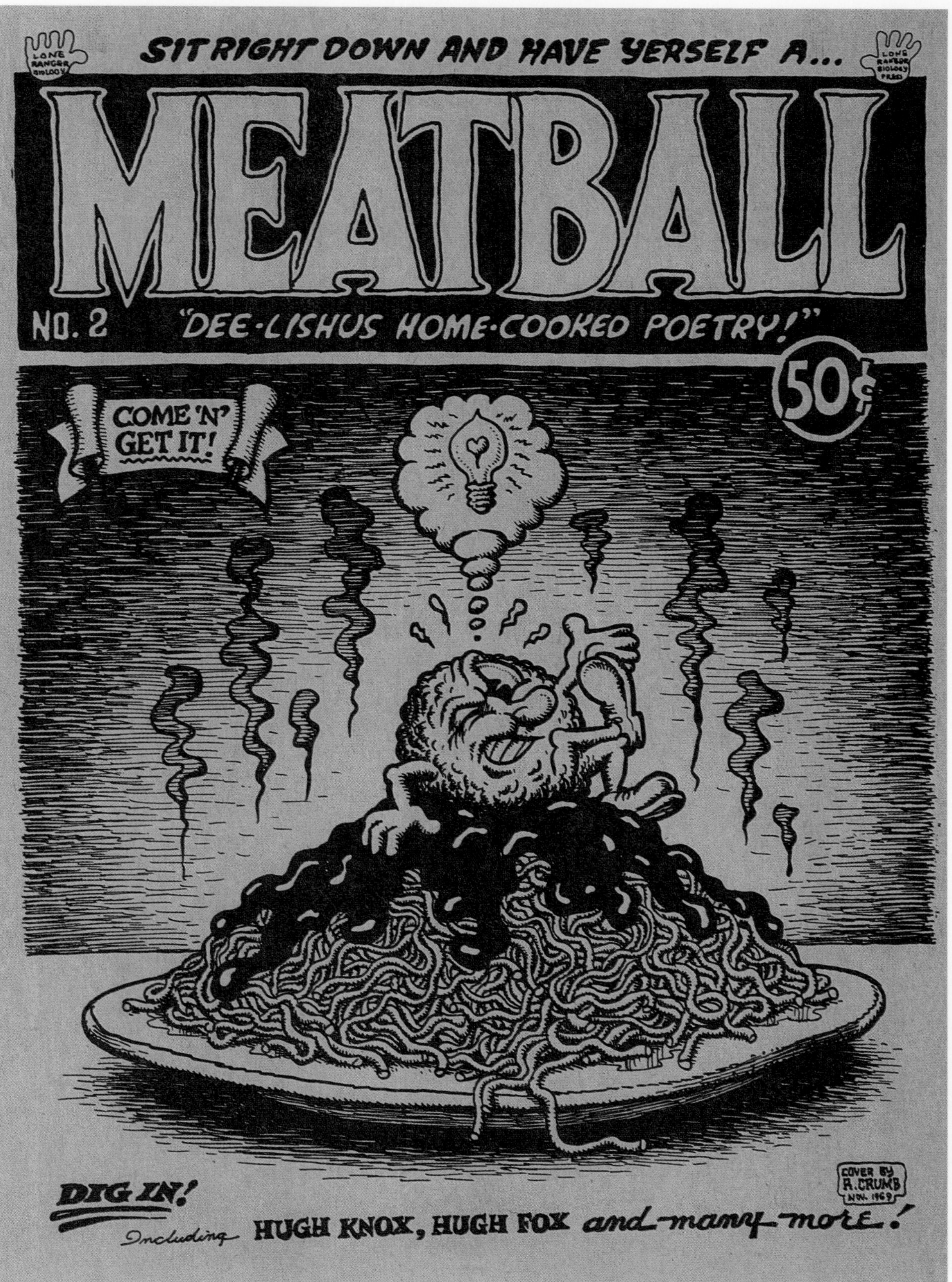

Cover of Meatball magazine, number 2, Lone Ranger Biology Press, Cambridge, Mass.

GRAB YOUR COAT AND GET YOUR HAT

LEAVE YOUR WORRIES ON THE DOORSTEP...

JUST DIRECT YOUR FEET TO THE SUNNY SIDE OF THE STREET...

DONTCHA HEAR THAT PITTER PAT?

THAT HAPPY TUNE IS YOUR STEP
LIFE CAN BE SO SWEET, ON THE SUNNY SIDE OF THE STREET!

I USED TO WALK IN THE SHADE...

WITH MY BLUES ON PARADE....

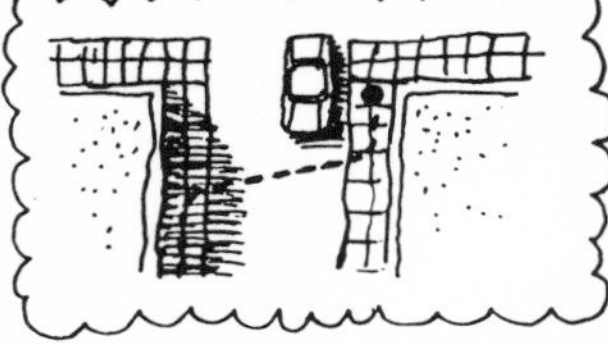
BUT NOW I'M NOT AFRAID, I'M A ROVER WHO CROSSED OVER...

AND IF I NEVER HAD A CENT....

I'D BE RICH AS ROCKE-FELLER...

GOLD DUST AT MY FEET... ON THE SUNNY SIDE OF THE STREET
R. Crumb

for Dana on her 24th Birthday December 6, 1969
from Robert with Love

Comic on the inside cover of Meatball magazine, number 2, Lone Ranger Biology Press, Cambridge, Mass.

Dana & Jesse, for Dana on her 24th birthday, from a photograph of Dana & Jesse.

John Gibbons on the Air, serial comic, made on request and added to an original résumé. Unpublished.

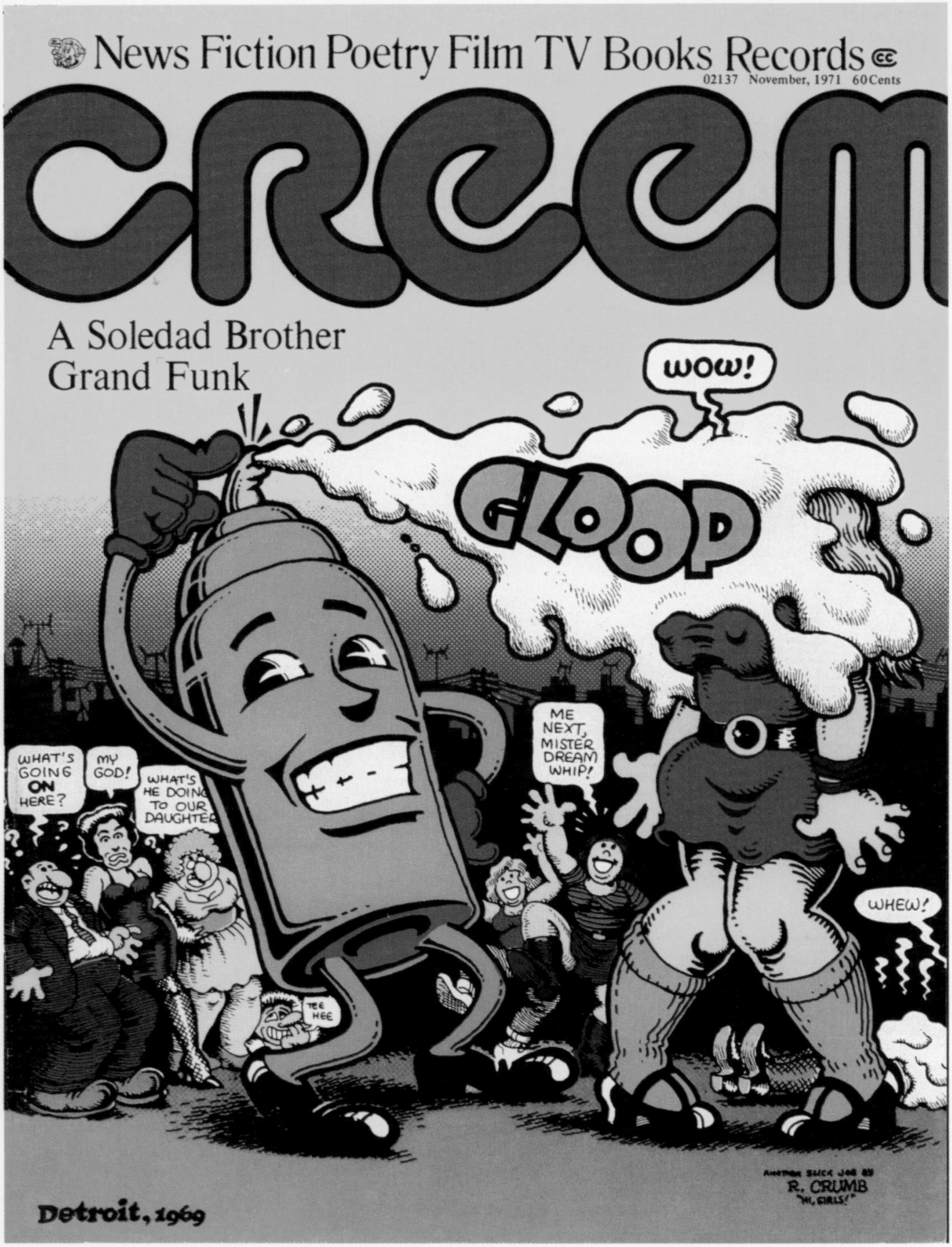

News Fiction Poetry Film TV Books Records

02137 November, 1971 60Cents

CREEM

A Soledad Brother
Grand Funk

WOW!

GLOOP

WHAT'S GOING ON HERE?

MY GOD!

WHAT'S HE DOING TO OUR DAUGHTER

ME NEXT, MISTER DREAM WHIP!

TEE HEE

WHEW!

ANOTHER SLICK JOB BY R. CRUMB "HI, GIRLS!"

Detroit, 1969

Cover of Creem magazine, number 2.

Cover of Creem magazine, number 2. Reprinted and colored in 1971.

Poster for a Robert Crumb exposition at Berkeley Gallery, San Francisco. 1970

Danie holding
Stanley & Oliver
- R. CRUMB
WITH LOVE

This Book is the
Personal Property
of:
MY BOOKS
JIGGLE
BOUNCE
5¢ per mile
AH'S BE PO' RELASHUN SO AH GITS TA RIDE FO' FREE!!
R. CRUMB

See...Hear...Feel...Taste...Smell
Go ahead, raise a few eyebrows.
THE east OTHER village
SPECIAL 5th ANNIVERSARY ISSUE
1965
1970
I JUST CAN'T GET LOOSE WITHOUT THAT JUICE
PHYSICAL HYGIENE MENTAL HEALTH AND MORAL RESPONSABILITY
BE AS SELFISH AS THE NEIGHBORHOOD YOU LIVE IN!
VOL 6 NO 1. DEC. 1, 1970 25¢ NYC 35¢ OUTSIDE

SOME PEOPLE THINK I'M CRAZY BECAUSE I BELIEVE IN CRAZY THINGS, BUT I DON'T CARE! I BELIEVE IN LEPRECHAUNS, FLYING SAUCERS, DRAGONS...
...AND YOU!

Danie Holding Stanley & Oliver, portrait, unpublished.

Book Plate, limited edition.

Special 5th Anniversary Issue, cover of The Each Village Other magazine, volume 6, number 1, Robert Crumb together with Spain Rodriguez, Robin Williams, Kim Deitch, Rory Hayes and Trina Robbins, New York.

Card, coverdrawing and inside text, American Greetings, Cleveland.

Cover, inside text and logo for 2 Valentine Cards, American Greetings, Cleveland.
1971

Portrait of Jesse Crumb, unpublished.
1971

...OR MAYBE BECAUSE OF THEM!

HAPPY VALENTINE'S DAY

MUSIC FANS!
HERE 'TIS!! A NEW CONCEPT IN RECORDED MUSIC!!
The Ordinary RECORD!
ORDINARY MUSIC FOR ORDINARY PEOPLE
HEY, SUZIE!! LOOK WHAT'S THE LATEST THING!! "RIVER BLUES" ON ONE SIDE AND "WISCONSIN WIGGLES" ON THE OTHER!!
OH WOW!! THOSE SOUND LIKE FAR-OUT SOUNDS!! I CAN'T WAIT TO PLAY IT! 78 RPM TOO!! HOW COOL!!
ORDINARY RECORD
THAT'S RIGHT! 78 RPM!! LOOK FOR THIS FIRST-IN-A-SERIES IN THE EXCITING REVIVAL OF "REGULAR" MUSIC!!! "RIVER BLUES" and "WISCONSIN WIGGLES" by R. Crumb and his Keep-on-Truckin' Orchestra
$1.50 EACH
(AVAILABLE BY MAIL ONLY FROM Krupp Comic Wks. P.O. BOX 5699, MILWAUKEE, 53211, WISCONSIN

GOLDEN GATE
PUBLISHING COMPANY
429 Brazil St., San Francisco, California 94112
(415) 585-3912
"WE ARE THE HIPPEST UNDERGROUND COMIX PUBLISHERS IN THE ENTIRE BAY AREA!"

EVERYTHING'S GONNA BE OKAY, AMERICA!!
SHAKE!
for Maggie from R. CRUMB © 1972
13TH ave. NATURAL·FOODS cafe @ 626 E. 13TH AVE. (BETWEEN WASHINGTON & PEARL) PHONE # 534-9192
HOURS: MONDAY THRU FRIDAY 11AM TO 9PM SATURDAY 3PM TO 9PM
CARRY OUT SERVICE

13TH AVE
CAFE
DINNERS
SANDWICHES
SALADS

Advertisement for The Ordinary Record, Krupp Comic Works, Milwaukee, Wis.

Golden Gate, letter-head for Golden Gate Publishing Company. (Terry Zwigoff & Kathy Goodell).

Everything's Gonna Be Okay, America!!, flyer for 13th Ave. Natural Foods Cafe, New York.

Illustrations for the menu of 13th Ave. Natural Foods Cafe, New York.

Woodman, Spare That Tree!, cover of The Mendocino Grapevine, a County Newspaper, number 2, Mendocino County, Ca. 1973

A NEW 78 RPM PHONOGRAPH RECORD BY

R. Crumb & his Keep~on~Truckin' Orchestra

RIVER BLUES/WISCONSIN WIGGLES

SOLD HERE

Ordinary Records

A division of Krupp Comic Works, Inc., P.O. Box 5699, Milwaukee, Wis. 53211

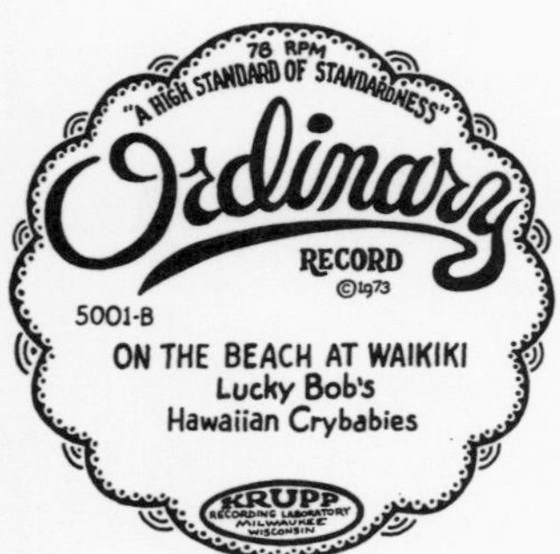

Small promotion poster, Ordinary Records, a division of Krupp Comic Works, Milwaukee, Wis.

Laughing Gas, Nitrous Oxide, book cover, And/Or Press.

Ordinary Record, logo, Krupp Recording Laboratory, Milwaukee, Wis.

Single sleeve design, Ordinary Record.

Sleeve design for Ordinary Record, printed on brown paper.

It's 'Red-Tag' Time in the Country!, cover of The Mendocino Grapevine, a County Newspaper, number 16, Mendocino County, Ca.
1974

for Dana with Love Robert Oct. 1974

TRICKS COMICS
2 BITS
25¢
HAVEN'T I SEEN YOU SOMEPLACE BEFORE?
PROBABLY... MAYBE ON T.V....
ARE YOU BUSY?
NEVER TOO BUSY, HONEY!
FEEL LIKE A PARTY? YOU SURE ARE A SEXY BITCH!!
WHAT KIND OF PARTY? YOU'RE NOT SO BAD YOURSELF, SUGAR!!
I'D MAKE IT WORTH YOUR WHILE... YOUR PLACE OR MINE?
OH YEAH, YOUR PLACE SOUNDS GOOD...
LET'S GO!
I'M SORRY BUT YOU'RE UNDER ARREST... OOPS!
TURK ST.
LARK
HOTEL
CLICK
CLICK
©1975 R.CRUMB
2ND NATIONAL HOOKERS CONVENTION
JUNE 21 · EXHIBIT HALL · HYATT REGENCY · SAN FRANCISCO

THE PRIEBE GALLERY
AND THE O.S.A. SPEAKERS AND O.S.A. CONCERT COMMITTEES
PRESENT AN OSHKOSH
CARTOON·O·RAMA!
FEATURING
A ONE-MAN SHOW BY WISCONSIN UNDERGROUND ARTIST
Denis Kitchen
PLUS A SEPARATE EXHIBIT FROM HIS COLLECTION,
"50 Years of Cartoons"
REPRESENTING THE TOP CARTOONISTS OF THE CENTURY
Feb. 5th–28th
IN THE PRIEBE GALLERY AND ANNEX. HOURS POSTED.
Harvey Kurtzman
CREATOR OF MAD, LITTLE ANNIE FANNY, ETC.
Fri. Feb. 20, 12:30 UNION LOUNGE
Midwest Debut!
R. Crumb
and his
CHEAP-SUIT SERENADERS
Sat. 8pm FEB. 21
AMERICA'S BEST KNOWN UNDERGROUND CARTOONIST NOW HAS A TOP-NOTCH STRING BAND... DON'T MISS THEM!! UNION "DRAFT BOARD"
DALE MESSICK
AWARD-WINNING "BRENDA STARR" ARTIST... ONE OF THE GREAT FEMALE CARTOONISTS.
Fri. FEB. 20 (TIME TO BE ANNOUNCED.)
PANEL
MODERATED BY PROF. BARRY WIND OF THE UWM ART HISTORY DEPT., FEATURING ALL THE ARTISTS ABOVE...
FRIDAY FEB. 20 7:30pm
UNION LOUNGE
BILL SANDERS
CAUSTIC EDITORIAL CARTOONIST FOR THE MILWAUKEE JOURNAL WILL GIVE A CHALK TALK
FRI. FEB. 20 (TIME TO BE ANNOUNCED)
Classic Animated Cartoons
all afternoon in Lounge, Sat. Feb. 21
UNIV. OF WIS. OSHKOSH

4
GUS CANNON ("BANJO JOE")
©1971 R. CRUMB

For Dana With Love, unpublished drawing.

Announcement poster for Cartoon-O-Rama.
1976

Four Arguments for the Elimination of Television, illustration for the Co-Evolution Quarterly.
1977

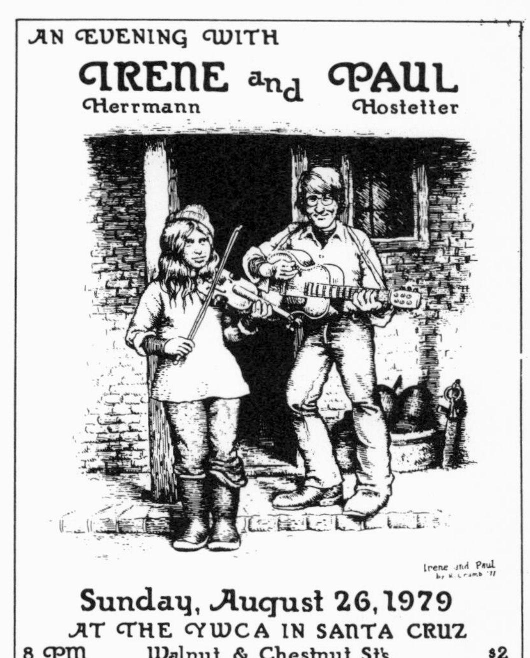

An Evening with Irene Herrmann and Paul Hostetter, invitation.
1977

Tricks Comics magazine, cover, Coyote, San Francisco.
1977

Gus Cannon ('Banjo Joe'), button, produced by Pinback Jack.
1977

Cover drawing for the publisher's catalogue, Zweitausendeins, Frankfurt a. M.
1978

MUSICIAN'S PARTY
SUNDAY, JUNE 24th, 1979
STARTS AT 1:00 P.M.
at
ZAMORA TOWN HALL
"POT LUCK"
WILL PUT ALL FOOD TOGETHER ON ONE TABLE.
BRING EITHER SALAD OR HOT DISH & DESSERT
& DRINKS. BRING PLATES, SILVERWARE & CUPS.
BRING YOUR MUSICAL INSTRUMENT

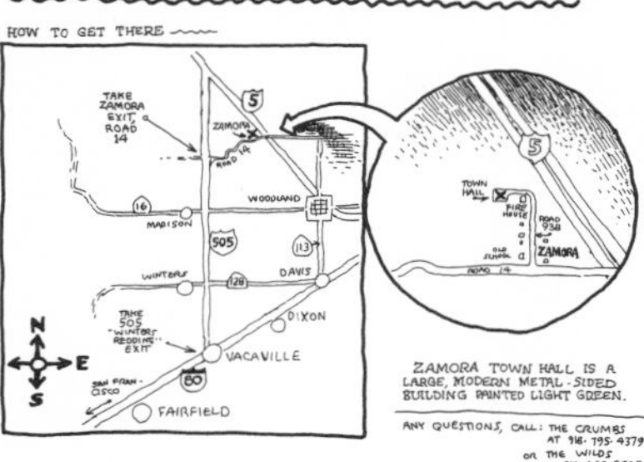

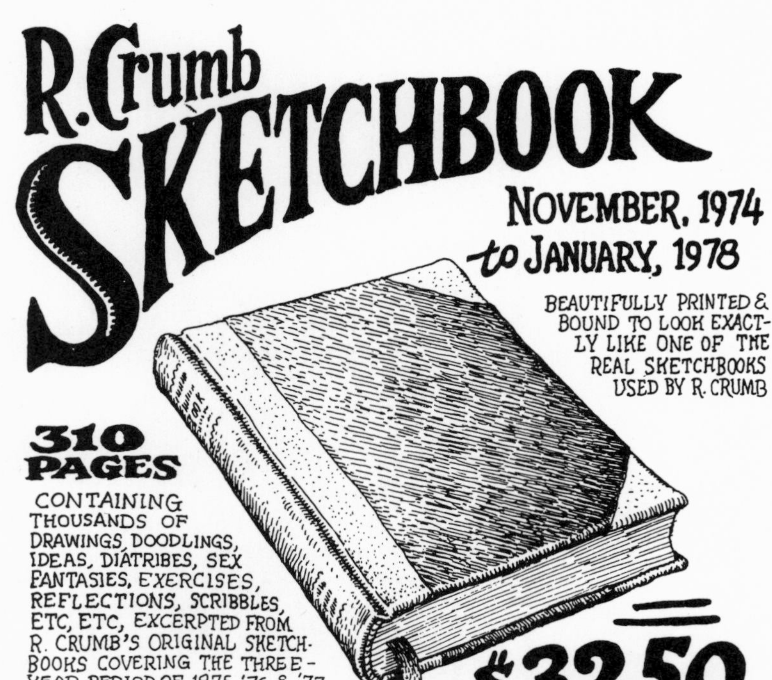

HOW TO GET THERE

ZAMORA TOWN HALL IS A LARGE, MODERN METAL-SIDED BUILDING PAINTED LIGHT GREEN.
ANY QUESTIONS, CALL: THE CRUMBS AT 916-795-4379

R. Crumb
SKETCHBOOK
NOVEMBER, 1974
to JANUARY, 1978
BEAUTIFULLY PRINTED & BOUND TO LOOK EXACTLY LIKE ONE OF THE REAL SKETCHBOOKS USED BY R. CRUMB
310 PAGES
CONTAINING THOUSANDS OF DRAWINGS, DOODLINGS, IDEAS, DIATRIBES, SEX FANTASIES, EXERCISES, REFLECTIONS, SCRIBBLES, ETC, ETC, EXCERPTED FROM R. CRUMB'S ORIGINAL SKETCHBOOKS COVERING THE THREE-YEAR PERIOD OF 1975, '76 & '77.
$32.50
POSTPAID
RIBBON BOOK MARK

A PERSONAL COMMENT BY R. CRUMB:

THERE'S ALOT OF VERY INTIMATE MATERIAL IN THIS BOOK. SOME OF IT IS EVEN EMBARRASSING FOR ME TO LOOK AT, LET ALONE ANYBODY ELSE. BUT I SUPPOSE YOU HAVE TO PUT IT OUT THERE, FOR BETTER OR WORSE. YOU COULD SAY MY LIFE IS AN OPEN BOOK, LITERALLY. IT'S ALL PRETTY SPONTANEOUS, PRETTY STREAM-OF-CONSCIOUSNESS IN THESE SKETCHBOOKS. YOU HAVE TO PUT IN SOME TIME DOING THAT WHEN YOUR WORK IS GENERALLY DONE FOR PRINT, FOR REPRODUCTION, OTHERWISE YOU MIGHT FALL INTO RIGID STYLISTIC RUTS, PREDICTABLE, ALL-TOO-FAMILIAR, BORING, DREARY, SUICIDE-INDUCING... ALOT OF CARTOONISTS WIND UP COMMITTING SUICIDE... THIS IS NO JOKE. SOMETHING ABOUT THE REPITITIOUSNESS OF THE JOB—DRAWING THOSE SAME LITTLE CHARACTERS IN THEIR SAME LITTLE BOXES YEAR AFTER YEAR... YOU HAVE TO KEEP TAPPING THE SUB-CONSCIOUS, YOU HAVE TO KEEP IT LOOSE, PLAYFUL. ALL YOUR NEW IDEAS, DISCOVERIES, INNOVATIONS COME WHEN YOU ARE CASUALLY DOODLING, FOOLING AROUND, NOT THINKING, NOT TAYING TO PLEASE "THEM". THAT'S WHAT'S IN THIS BOOK. NONE OF IT WAS EVER DONE INTENTIONALLY FOR PUBLICATION, BUT THEY TELL ME PEOPLE LIKE TO SEE THAT SIDE OF IT, TOO, SO HERE 'TIS!

Made in West Germany by "2001" Publishing Company, it is now being imported only by Bélier Press

from
BELIER PRESS
P.O. BOX "C"
GRACIE STATION
NEW YORK, N.Y. 10028

CAROL ENGBERG
"MISS SUPPLY DISPOSAL" OF 1979

— R. CRUMB
JAN., 1979

Musician's Party, flyer for a musician's party organized by the Crumb & Wild families.

Pottery designs, made for a woman potter who intended to use them for ceramic cups and boxes. The project was never completed.

Carol Engberg, 'Miss Supply Disposal of 1979', unpublished.

R. Crumb Sketchbook, flyer/advertisement, Belier Press, New York.

...AND SO, MY FRIENDS...

Mr.Natural

©R. CRUMB

Calling card for Wally Summ Music Studio.

Calling card for Professor Gizmo.

WALLY SUMM MUSIC STUDIO
666-1024

Quality Instruction
—ON—
GUITAR · FIDDLE
BANJO · VIOLIN
MANDOLIN · BASS

RT. 3, BOX 845 * WOODLAND, CA 95695

Professor Gizmo

ONE MAN BAND

(Rick Elmore)

29 El Camino Drive
Corte Madera, CA 94925

(415) 927-7808

Possum Trot String Band

CLASSICAL RECORDS

Thanksgiving in the Valley, illustration for Winds of Change magazine, Yolo County, Ca.

Magazine illustration ('Dancercize'), The Winters Express, Ca.

Calling card for Kippy Original, San Francisco, Ca.

Logo Bélier Press, New York.

Illustration for an article on computers in the Co-Evolution Quarterly.

Flyer for the Second Annual Musician's Party at Zamora Town Hall, organized by the Crumb & Wild families.

King of the Freaks, portrait of Johnny Eck, Anaconda Press.

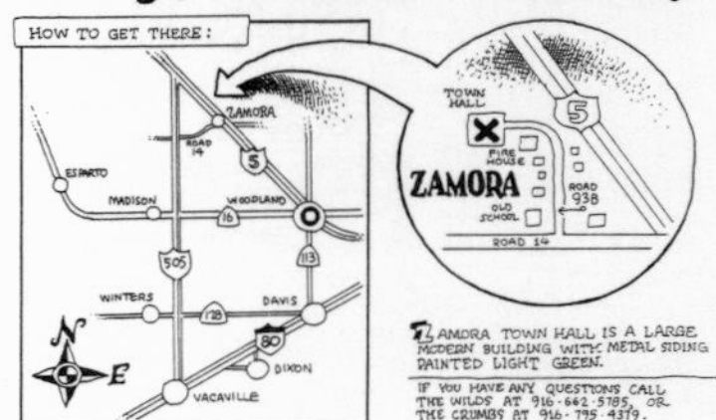

Calling card for the Possum Trot String Band.

Illustration for a calling card for J.B. Rund.

Calling card (reverse side) for J.B. Rund.

CAR CITY RECORDS

I GOTTA HAVE MY MUSIC!

R. CRUMB

21918 HARPER AVENUE
ST. CLAIR SHORES, MICHIGAN 48080

Car City Records, design for a record store (with J.B. Rund as a partner) in a Detroit suburb.

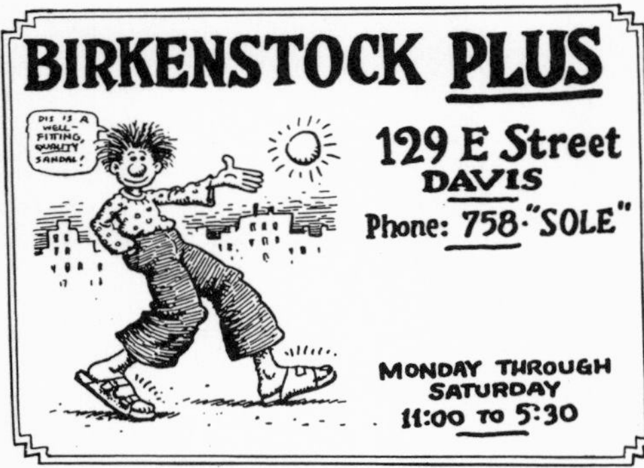

Illustrations for Winds of Change, Yolo County, Ca.

Vol. II, No. 1. YOLO COUNTY, CALIFORNIA July, 1980

PRICE: 75 CENTS

FIRST ISSUE FREE!

AGRI-BU$INE$$ JUGGERNAUT

FUEL TANK

I THINK WE BETTER GET ORGANIZED!

HIGH IDEALS

LI'L OL' LABOR SAVERS

R. CRUMB 1980

"Know Thine Enemy!"

1980

Cover of Winds of Change, volume II, number 1, Yolo County, Ca.

Illustrations for Winds of Change, Yolo County, Ca. 1980-1981

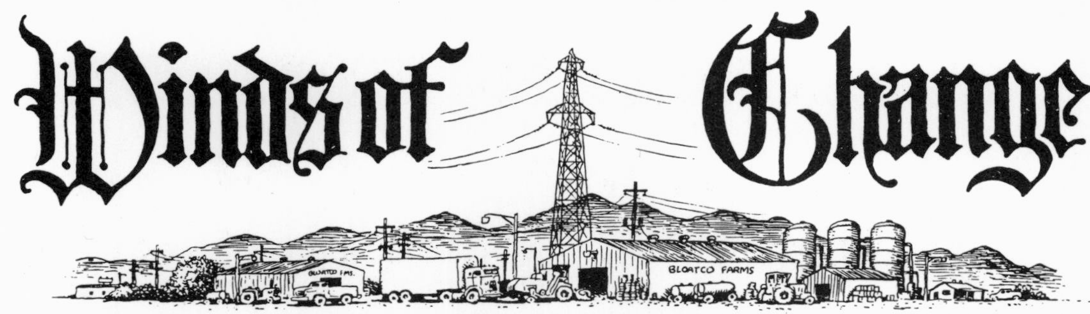

VOL. II, No. 2 YOLO COUNTY, CALIFORNIA August, 1980

PRICE: 50 CENTS

Ag Biz Juggernaut Defined
Knight's Landing Visit
Yolo Gossip Column!
Winters Zapped by "Progress"
Ethanol: Big Stills vs. Small
Welfare Forced-Work Program

Railroad Car Community in Winters

Progress in Winters?
The New Community Center

By Aline Kominsky-Crumb

I remember the first time I came to Winters. I drove over the old bridge and to the right was a wonderful little community of railroad cars. It was a perfect small universe: a cozy, intimate area with the right combination of funkiness and order. The grounds were well kept and lush, the railroad cars brightly painted, and there was a fenced-in yard for chickens. The feeling of this place made me want to move to Winters.

It told me that Winters was a relaxed community that hadn't been exploited yet by out of town schlock* developers. I thought "Winters still has a heart and soul ... it's a good town." Basically, I still think this is true, but the forces of economic greed are at work here. Now when I drive over the bridge into town, I see an imposing building, surrounded by a sea of asphalt, looming over the humble railroad cars. One railroad car has been removed for a parking lot and the fate of the remaining ones is uncertain.

Quite often people do not value the intangible richness in the quality of their lives until it changes. It seems to happen suddenly. It is however, a process. Modernization and becoming part of the mono-culture is sold to us, promising us a more prosperous future. The merchants are told that the town has to grow in order to just survive. We bend to the power of the mighty buck. A few people and companies make a profit. In the end we lose the uniqueness of the place we live.

A long-time Winters resident told me that she had always intended to do a painting of the railroad cars. It was her favorite place. Now the feeling of that area is totally changed.

I like the idea of a Winters Community Center. The building represents volunteer work and a deep sense of community spirit. Raising funds was a formidable struggle and the people succeeded. It is too bad that they settled for the existing building. In the end, they were sadly shortchanged.

Unfortunately, the Community Center is not an energy-efficient building. It has a dark tile roof plus inadequate wall and ceiling insulation. This is contrary to recommendations made by the Winters Energy Commission. They studied the problems of energy use and found that it is economical to upgrade insulation and downsize heating and cooling units. The amount saved increases greatly in a large building like the Community Center. A member of this commission told me that the Center was built with little regard to energy use. He said the monthly operating costs are really part of the total cost of the building. In this case the heating and cooling costs alone (estimated by two knowledgeable people) would be around $200 a month. Also, more foliage than they have allotted space for could have significantly dropped indoor temperature.

Other designs were submitted to the city. Living Systems' design utilized solar heat, natural cooling, and a surrounding park incorporating the railroad cars. This plan and the idea of an energy efficient building in general, were rejected by the city, despite the fact that Living Systems obtained grant money for a solar building. It's almost as though the people in power are afraid of conservation. They seem to think it's part of some "communist plot coming out of Davis." This is unfortunate because we all pay for this waste. It is interesting to note that a paid PG&E employee heads the design committee and has played an integral part in the outcome of the Community Center. It is thought provoking to wonder why PG&E is involved in this kind of activity.

Another negative aspect of the Community Center is its insensitive placement. It is no more than 10 feet from the railroad car community, and it is uncomfortably close to many poor people's cabins. These poor people have no power and are not considered important enough to worry about. They can simply be relocated when they get in the way. One of the reasons behind the placement of the building is an alleged need for more parking space in the downtown area. This theory is based on the results of a report done in 1978 called the Central Business Area Plan. An outside firm was hired by the city with H.U.D. grant money to figure out why downtown business wasn't doing well.

(Continued on p. 8

*schlock-a Yiddish word meaning a shoddy, cheaply made article, a defective or fake item, a gyp.

Cover of Winds of Change, volume II, number 2, Yolo County, Ca.

HALLOWE'EN EDITION

Winds of Change

Vol. II, No. 4 | YOLO COUNTY, CALIFORNIA | October, 1980

25¢

"**WARNING!** KEEP OUT OF REACH OF CHILDREN. CAUSES EYE IRRITATION. AVOID CONTACT WITH EYES. HARMFUL IF SWALLOWED. WASH THOROUGHLY AFTER HANDLING. PROLONGED OR REPEATED INHALATION OF VAPOR OR SKIN CONTACT WITH SPRAY MAY BE HARMFUL."

—Herbicide Label

GIVE A GIFT SUBSCRIPTION AND HELP US MAKE 500 BY NEW YEAR'S!

GOAL

IT'S A FUN ZONE, RIGHT?

Cover of Winds of Change, Hallowe'en Edition, volume II, number 4, Yolo County, Ca.

Illustrations for Winds of Change, Yolo County, Ca. 1980-1981

Vol. II, No. 6 — YOLO COUNTY, CALIFORNIA — December-January, 1980-81

25¢

PARTY TIME BEER

BAH HUMBUG!

R. CRUMB '80

Merry Christmas!
from Mr. Appropriate and his minions

Cover of Winds of Change, Christmas Edition, volume II, number 6, Yolo County, Ca.

GET YOUR
WINDS T-SHIRT
DRAWN BY R. CRUMB
WHILE THEY LAST!
HEY! I'M COOL!
(REG $6.00)
HALF-OFF
WITH A SUBSCRIPTION TO "WINDS OF CHANGE"
WINDS of CHANGE
A
SUPPLY LIMITED
T-SHIRT and SUBSCRIPTION: $13.00 REG.
$13.50 FRENCH CUT
REG. SUBSCRIPTION - $10.00
T-SHIRT SHOWS YOUR FRIEND AND OURS: "MR. APPROPRIATÉ"!!
MAIL ORDERS PLEASE STATE SIZE: S, M, L OR XL AND STYLE DESIRED.

COMMUNITY CANNERY
CLOSED
R. CRUMB

letters
HEH HEH

Written on the Winds

Yolo Gardens

SALE

WIND POWERED TOOTH BRUSH
SOLAR REFLECTOR POWERED TAPE DECK
TODAY ECOTOPIA TOMORROW THE WORLD PEACE!

Senior Soapbox

BEAT IT
NOBODY LIKES ME ANYMORE!

BACK TO THE DRAWING BOARD

Illustrations for Winds of Change, Yolo County, Ca.

HEY, LET'S FACE IT—IT GIVES PEOPLE JOBS!

Illustrations for Winds of Change, Yolo County, Ca.

Vol II, No. 7 | YOLO COUNTY, CALIFORNIA | February, 1981

25¢

Survival in the Suburbs:

The Backyard
at Isao's
House
January, 1981
by R. Crumb

Towards a More Efficient Use of Space

Cover of Winds of Change, volume II, number 7, Yolo County, Ca.

APRIL FOOL EDITION

WINDS OF CHANGE

VOL 2, NO. 9 YOLO COUNTY, CALIFORNIA APRIL 1ST, 1981

25¢

Cover of Winds of Change,
April Fool Edition,
volume II, number 9,
Yolo County, Ca.

Vol. III, No. 1 — YOLO COUNTY, CALIFORNIA — September, 1981

BUZZ
SQUAWK
YAK YAK SHREEK
GRONK
DING DONG!
BUZZZT!
BOING!
DAILY NEWS
GETCHA PAPEH!
Winds of Change
R. CRUMB '81

He's little but he packs a wallop!

Cover of Winds of Change,
volume III, number 1,
Yolo County, Ca.

TO RYE
CAROL ENGBERG
IN HER POP-ART BATHING
SUIT.

Self-portrait. Publication unknown.

Reflections by a Farming Woman, illustration for the Co-Evolution Quarterly.

Crayon drawings, made while drawing with Sophie. 1984

Pepper & Stern Rare Books Inc., promotion poster. 1984

Christmas card for the McNamara family.

Carol Engberg in her pop-art bathing suit.

Illustrations for an article in the Co-Evolution Quarterly, called Meetings with Remarkable Cat Ladies. 1984

"HE'S SO DICK-FINGERED HE CAN'T PICK HIS NOSE WITHOUT PUTTIN' HIS EYE OUT."

"ASS LIKE A BLACK WIDOW SPIDER'S"

--R. CRUMB

"YOU BUY 'EM BOOKS AND YOU BUY 'EM BOOKS AND THEY JUST CHEW ON THE COVERS."

"NEVER HIRE A MAN WHO WEARS A STRAW HAT, SMOKES ROLL-YOUR-OWN CIGARETTES OR WEARS LACE-UP BOOTS."

"LOOKS LIKE A MONKEY TRYING TO FUCK A FOOTBALL."

AAARNNHH
"I NEVER SEEN A MAN GET SO HONKED OFF OVER A LOUSY POOL GAME!"

1984

CRUMB

Loose in the Streets, comic made by Robert Crumb together with O'Neill, Moscoso and Crabman for S.F. Chronicle.

Illustrations for Texas Crude, A Few Philosophical Illustrations, E.P. Dutton Inc., New York.

"UGLY AS DEATH BACKING OUT OF A SHITHOUSE READING MAD MAGAZINE."

"I WAS SO MAD AT MY WIFE I SAT ON THE SIDE OF THE BED AND JACKED OFF JUST TO SHOW MY INDEPENDENCE!"

R. CRUMB

"BELT BUCKLE POLISHER"

Illustrations for Texas Crude, A Few Philosophical Illustrations, E.P. Dutton Inc., New York.

"HE COULDN'T GET A PIECE OF ASS IN A WHOREHOUSE WITH A FISTFUL OF FIFTY-DOLLAR BILLS."

"TRACER BOOGER"

Illustrations for Texas Crude, A Few Philosophical Illustrations, E.P. Dutton Inc., New York.

Texas Crude, book cover, E.P. Dutton Inc., New York.

Look What We Harvested!! Birth announcement card for the McNamara family.

Baby Shower, invitation card for Julie McNamara

The Monkey Wrench Gang, book cover printed on back of 1986 calendar, Dream Garden Press, Salt Lake City, Utah.

Illustrations for The Monkey Wrench Gang, calendar, Dream Garden Press, Salt Lake City, Utah. Appeared also in a book with the same title. Calendar published in 1986.

"In the lurid glare which followed he could be seen shambling back to the Lincoln Continental Mark IV parked nearby, empty gas can banging on his insouciant shanks."

"They worked happily. Hard hats clinked and clanked against the steel. Lines and rods snapped apart with the rich *spang!* and solid *clunk!* of metal severed under tension. Doc lit another stogie. Smith wiped a drop of oil from his eyelid."

"AS THE TIPOVER POINT APPROACHED THE TRACTOR ATTEMPTED (SO IT SEEMED) TO SAVE ITSELF: ONE TREAD BEING MORE ADVANCED INTO THE AIR THAN THE OTHER, THE TRACTOR MADE A LURCHING HALF-TURN TO THE RIGHT, TRYING TO CLING TO THE RIM OF THE MESA AND SOMEHOW REGAIN SOLID FOOTING."

"THERE WAS AN ANGUISHED CRUNCH OF STEEL AS THE BLAZER, SQUIRTING VITAL INTERNAL JUICES IN ALL DIRECTIONS...SANK AND DISAPPEARED BENEATH THE UNSPEAKABLE IMPACT, WHEELS SPREAD-EAGLED, BODY CRUSHED LIKE A BUG."

"YOU CAN'T NEVER GO WRONG CUTTIN' FENCE," REPEATED SMITH, WARMING TO HIS TASK. "ALWAYS CUT FENCE. THAT'S THE LAW WEST OF THE HUNDREDTH MERIDIAN...."

"SOME TOURISTS STOPPED TO STARE AT SMITH; ONE RAISED A CAMERA. HAYDUKE, STANDING GUARD, PUT A HAND ON THE POMMEL OF HIS SHEATHED KNIFE AND GLARED. THEY WENT AWAY."

Illustrations for The Monkey Wrench Gang, calendar, Dream Garden Press, Salt Lake City, Utah. Appeared also in a book with the same title.

"HI," SAID HAYDUKE, GRINNING. "I'M A HIPPIE." HE SWUNG FOR THE STOMACH; THE COWBOY STAGGERED BACK AGAINST THE WALL. HAY-DUKE FACED THE FIVE OTHER COWBOYS AT THE TABLE. THEY WERE RISING TOO, ALL SMILES."

ALL OF A SUDDEN IT WAS ALL TOO MUCH. HE DREW BACK HIS BIG BOOTED RIGHT FOOT AND KICKED THE PICTURE TUBE SQUARE IN THE EYE."

"THE DIRECTOR WAS MONOCULAR. THE RED BEAM OF ITS UNLIDDED CYCLOPS EYE PLAYED ON THE FACE OF SELDOM SEEN, SCANNING HIS BRAIN, HIS NERVES, HIS SOUL. PARALYZED BY THAT HYPNOTIC RAY, SMITH WAITED HELPLESS AS A BABE."

"THE STEAM SPIRALED UP FROM THE COFFEE IN THE SHAPE, TRANSIENT BUT CLEAR, OF A QUESTION MARK. THE QUESTION WAS NOT THE PRACTICAL ONE—ARE THEY ARMED?.....THE QUESTION WAS: WILL THE SPHINCTER HOLD TILL I GET OUT OF HERE FREE AND CLEAR?"

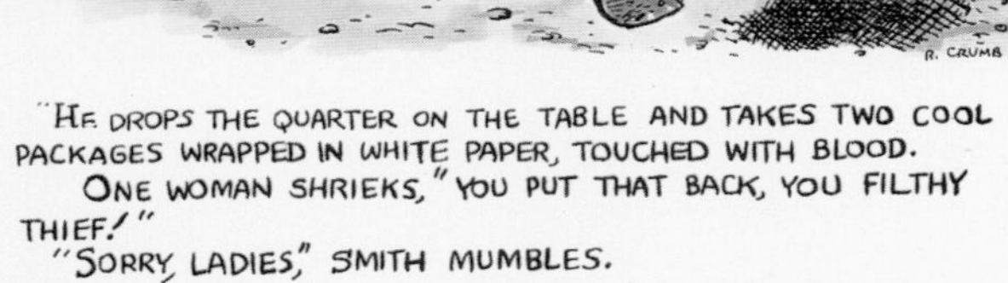

"HE DROPS THE QUARTER ON THE TABLE AND TAKES TWO COOL PACKAGES WRAPPED IN WHITE PAPER, TOUCHED WITH BLOOD.
ONE WOMAN SHRIEKS, "YOU PUT THAT BACK, YOU FILTHY THIEF!"
"SORRY, LADIES," SMITH MUMBLES.

"GOOD GOD, DOC THINKS. AND THEN REALIZES THAT HE IS NOT REALLY SURPRISED, THAT HE HAS BEEN EXPECTING THIS APPARITION FOR TWO YEARS. HE SIGHS. HERE WE GO AGAIN."

Illustrations for The Monkey Wrench Gang, calendar, Dream Garden Press, Salt Lake City, Utah. Appeared also in a book with the same title. Calendar published in 1986.

I'M HAVING A BLAST THIS CHRISTMAS!!
HAVE A HAPPY HOLIDAY
from ROBERT,

PIRANHA
KA-BOOM
BUZZZZ
CRACKLE
BLEEP
BLOOP
BLIP
R. CRUMB '84

THE JOB MARKET
GOOD TO HAVE YOU WITH US, B-102-4336!
THANKS, J. B.
AW, C'MON, YOU GOTTA BE KIDDING— AWP!!
BASH
R. CRUMB '84

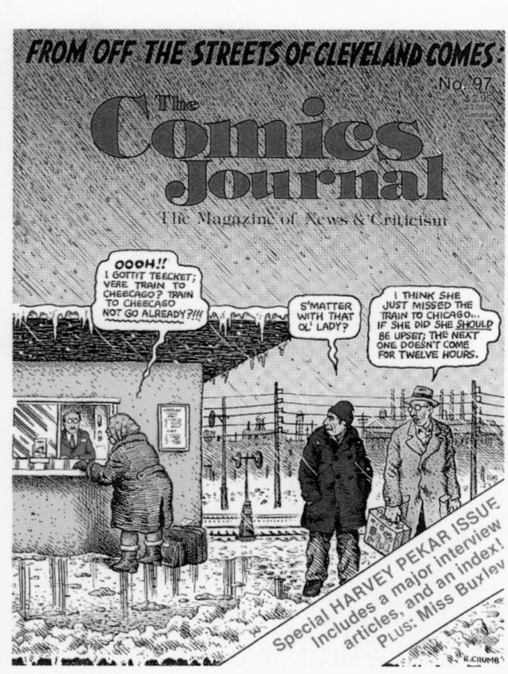
FROM OFF THE STREETS OF CLEVELAND COMES:
No. 97
The Comics Journal
The Magazine of News & Criticism
OOOH!! I GOTTIT TEECKET; VERE TRAIN TO CHEECAGO? TRAIN TO CHEECAGO NOT GO ALREADY?!!!
S'MATTER WITH THAT OL' LADY?
I THINK SHE JUST MISSED THE TRAIN TO CHICAGO... IF SHE DID SHE SHOULD BE UPSET; THE NEXT ONE DOESN'T COME FOR TWELVE HOURS.
Special HARVEY PEKAR ISSUE
Includes a major interview
articles, and an index!
PLUS: Miss Buxley
R. CRUMB

R. CRUMB '85

Have a Happy Holiday, card from the Crumb family.

Illustrations for Whole Earth Review.
1985

Crumb's on the Road, poster for 1985 European tour, Pictanium, The Pictish Cultural Society, Edinburgh, Scotland.
1985

Cover of The Comics Journal, number 97, Fantagraphics Books, Seattle.

Hinckle Free at Last, poster.
1985

Pumping Gas, illustration for a poem by Diane Callum for a local women's poetry magazine, Davis, Ca.
1985

Calling card for Julie Partansky.
1985

Calling card drawing for Terry Zwigoff.
1985

PICTANIUM, THE PICTISH CULTURAL SOCIETY
PRESENTS
Crumb's on the Road

PUMPING GAS by DIANE CALLUM

Stenciling
Wallpapering
Painting
Julie Partansky
916·753·3936

1954: LITTLE BOBBY CRUMB & HIS BROTHER CHUCK, A COUPLE OF COMIC-BOOK WIMPS
C'MON YOU GUYS! LET'S GO OUT 'N' TOSS TH' OL' PIGSKIN AROUND!
NAH... I DON'T FEEL LIKE IT, DAD...
WE'RE READING COMICS...

1967: R. CRUMB LEAVES CLEVELAND, JOINS THE HIPPY MIGRATION TO SAN FRANCISCO...
HOT DANG! MAYBE I'LL GET IN ON SOME O' THIS FREE LOVE STUFF!
STONED
TURN ON TUNE IN DROP OUT!
OH WOW!
SHANGRI-LA OR A BUST, MAN

R. CRUMB IN 1985... A REGULAR FAMILY KINDA GUY....
HEY, C'MON BOB... YOU TOO SOPH... LET'S GO FOR A HIKE!
NAH...I DON'T FEEL LIKE IT...
HEY LOOK DAD! THIS'S A BLIB... SEE?
©R. CRUMB 1985

GOODSTUFF
WINTERS, CALIFORNIA
306 RAILROAD AVE., 95694 (916-795-4636)

Good
R. CRUMB '85

Superior
PICTURES

PSSST! HEY! C'MERE! I GOT SOMETHIN' I WANNA TELL YA!!
THE MAGAZINE IZ MOVIN'!!

Autobiography cartoons drawn for Peoples magazine.

Drawing for Goodstuff, Winters, Ca.

Promotion card for The Magazine, presumably a second-hand magazines shop in San Francisco.

Letter-head for Superior Pictures (Terry Zwigoff).

Illustrations to Quest for Firewood, by Jay Feldman, Hightimes Magazine.

The Riley Sisters, portrait made in Edinburgh, Scotland.

Famous People I Have Known
Dew Drop Inn
Coors BEER
Ed McClanahan

"I DON'T TAKE TIPS SO HOW COULD I BE SOLICITING??"
R. CRUMB '85

DON'T WORRY, EVERYTHING'S GOING TO BE FINE....
YEAH SURE...

Season's Greetings
...and a Happy New Year!
R. CRUMB '85

Book cover: Famous People I Have Known, by Ed McClanahan.

Marilyn Chambers at the O'Farrell Theatre, San Francisco. Requested by the Mitchell brothers, operators of this porn & nude dancing theatre.

Portrait of Mary at Putah Creek, drawn from a photograph.

Mary, portrait.

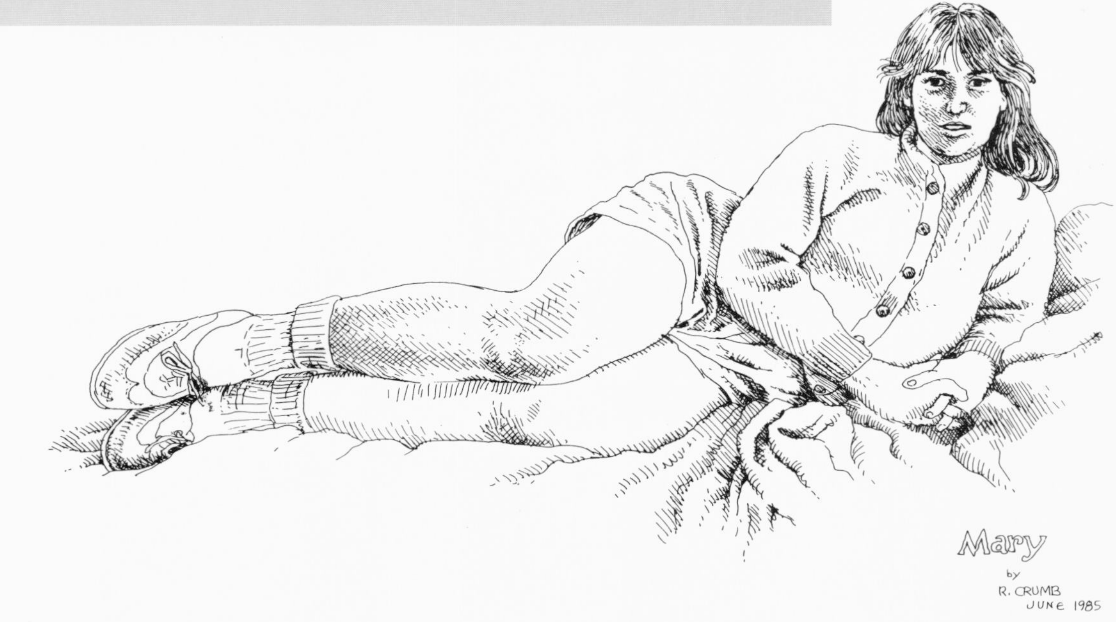

Don't Worry, Everything's Going to Be Fine, card based upon a silk-screen print.

Season's Greetings and a Happy New Year, card for the McNamara family.

Letter-head for Kitchen Sink Press, Northampton, Mass.

"ME N' MY MUSE"
by R. "MR. TERRIFIED-OF-EVERYTHING" CRUMB, PARIS, 1986
"LA HUNE" EXPOSE DES DESSINS ORIGINAUX DE ROBERT CRUMB DU 3 MARS AU 3 AVRIL 1986...
VOUS ÊTES INVITÉ A FÊTER CELA LE JEUDI 6 MARS '86... A PARTIR DE 18 H...
SNAP
LA HUNE
170 BOULEVARD
SAINT GERMAIN
75006 PARIS
TEL : 45·48·35·85

R. CRUMB '86

SAN FRANCISCO COMIX
$2.00
EGGS ACKLEY
NO. 8
A SAN FRANCISCO S.F. COMIX U.C.W.A
AWK
I FOUND YOU AMUSING FOR AWHILE, PUNK, BUT NOW I'M TIRED OF YOUR PATHETIC LITTLE EGO!
HA HA HA!
DAYTONA BEACH HEALTH CLUB
R. CRUMB JUNE '86

LAST GASP ECO-FUNNIES
$2.50
ARE YOU ONE OF THE UNDESIRABLES? ...THEN YOU MUST READ...
WEIRDO
NO. 18
HEY LEMME STICK THIS BANANA IN YER DONUT, OKAY?
OH MY GOSH! IT SURE IS A TIGHT FIT, HUH?! WOW!
KIDS! FIND THE HIDDEN MESSAGE!
© R. CRUMB '86

Me 'n' My Muse, invitation, La Hune bookstore, Paris, France.

Portrait of Mary Boettcher.

It's Been a Hell of a Year!, Christmas card drawn in December by Aline, Sophie and Robert Crumb.

Promotion card for Black Sparrow Press, Santa Rosa, Ca.

Cover of San Francisco Comix, number 8. Drawn on request and on the spot in Gary Arlington's comic bookstore. Gary Arlington's Small Publication, San Francisco.

Cover of Weirdo, number 18, Last Gasp Eco-Funnies, Berkely, Ca.

A Son..., birth announcement card, Karen and Thomas Arons.

Let's Get It Straight: It's a Girl, Born August 25th., inside birth announcement card, Karen and Thomas Arons.

Portrait of Mary Boettcher.

IT'S BEEN A HELL OF A YEAR!
BORN TO RAISE HELL
DRAWN IN DECEMBER, 1986 BY ALINE, SOPHIE & ROBERT CRUMB
Merry Christmas and Happy New Year
FROM BOB AND HIS DEVIL GIRLS

LET'S GET IT STRAIGHT: IT'S A GIRL, BORN AUGUST 25TH, 1986, 8:16 P.M.... 8 POUNDS, 13 OUNCES, 20 INCHES LONG... NAMED
ABIGAIL ROSE OLSON ARONS!
HM

The 1987
MONKEY WRENCH GANG
CALENDAR
by EDWARD ABBEY and R. CRUMB

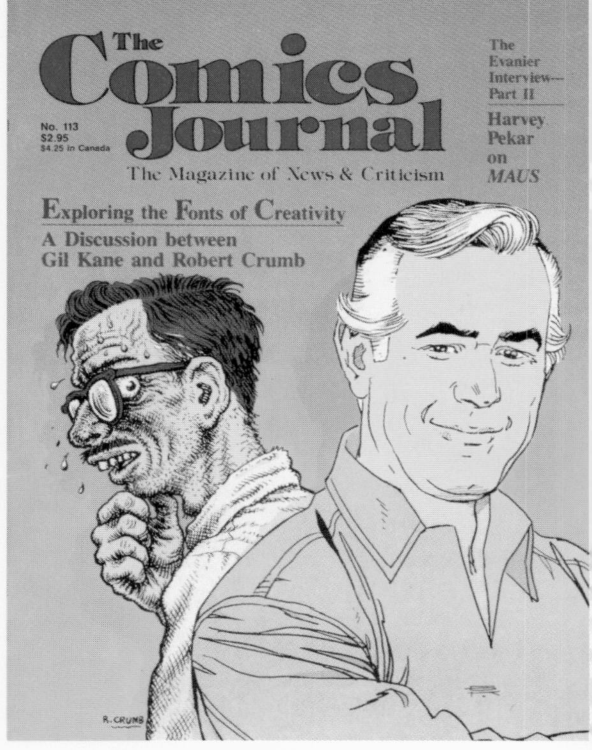
The
Comics
Journal
No. 113
$2.95
$4.25 in Canada
The Magazine of News & Criticism
The
Evanier
Interview—
Part II
Harvey
Pekar
on
MAUS
Exploring the Fonts of Creativity
A Discussion between
Gil Kane and Robert Crumb
R. CRUMB

Cover of The 1987 Monkey Wrench Gang Calendar, Dream Garden Press, Salt Lake City, Utah.

Title page drawings of The 1987 Monkey Wrench Gang Calendar, Dream Garden Press, Salt Lake City, Utah.

Crayon drawing, made while drawing with Sophie.

Dirtbag Bunny, crayon drawing, made while drawing with Sophie.

Exploring the Fonts of Creativity, cover of The Comics Journal, number 113, with Gil Kane, Fantagraphics Books, Seattle.

We Wish You a Merry Christmas, card made for the McNamara family.

Portrait of Margaret Thatcher on the front page of the French daily Libération.

R.CRUMB AU SALON INTERNATIONAL DE LA BANDE DESSINÉE D'

ANGOULÊME

OH MON DIEU! UNE JOLIE FILLE QUI LIT UN ALBUM DE B.D.!

...DU JAMAIS VU AUX U.S.A.!!

SOUS L'ATTAQUE DES MEDIAS
HE, JE DOIS ÊTRE UN PERSONNAGE IMPORTANT!

LES CAMERAS ET LES MICROS ME TERRORISENT ET IL Y EN AVAIT DES TAS À ANGOULÊME... POUR ME DÉFENDRE, JE LES DESSINAIS TANDIS QU'ON LES DIRIGEAIT SUR MOI... CE DESSIN EST UN ÉCHANTILLON DE CEUX QUE J'AI VUS

DES TAS DE BONNES B.D. A RAMENER A LA MAISON.... FRANÇAISES, ITALIENNES, ESPAGNOLES, BELGES....

INCROYABLE!
J'SUIS IMPRESSIONNÉ!

EN TRAIN DE FAIRE DES DESSINS POUR LES GENS.

Angoulême, Jan., 1986

LE SALON DE LA BANDE DESSINÉE D'ANGOULÊME A ÉTÉ UNE FORMIDABLE EXPÉRIENCE POUR MOI. VRAIMENT... J'AI FRÉQUENTÉ QUELQUES UNS DE CES EVÈNEMENTS AUX ETATS UNIS, MAIS ÇA N'AVAIT RIEN À VOIR.... L'ATMOSPHÈRE DE FÊTE DANS TOUTE LA VILLE LA FOULE, L'HOMMAGE RENDU AUX ARTISTES, ET LES FEMMES!! TOUTES CES FEMMES SUPERBES!! ON NE VOIT JAMAIS ÇA DANS LES "COMIX CON" AMÉRICAINES!! DES FEMMES À LA MODE, EN CUIR NOIR, CHAUSSÉES DE MAGNIFIQUES CHAUSSURES À HAUTS TALONS! DES FILLES FABULEUSES EN BLUE JEANS SERRÉS... HAUTAINES ET FIÈRES... PAR CENTAINES, DANS TOUS LES COINS... ET, OH OUI, LES BANDES DESSINÉES ÉTAIENT TRÈS BIEN AUSSI....

CES FANS DE BANDE DESSINÉE FRANÇAIS M'AIMAIENT À MORT... J'AI BOUSILLÉ MON RAPIDOGRAPHE À FAIRE DES DESSINS POUR CES CASSE-PIEDS EXIGEANTS, MAIS JE SUPPOSE QUE ÇA VAUT MIEUX QUE D'ÊTRE IGNORÉ.

PIERRE PASCAL — DIRECTEUR DU SALON

M. PASCAL, QUI SEMBLAIT ÊTRE LE RESPONSABLE DE TOUTE L'AFFAIRE, ÉTAIT PARTOUT À LA FOIS. J'AI RÉUSSI À FAIRE CE PORTRAIT DE LUI PENDANT UNE PAUSE DE DEUX MINUTES DANS LA CAVALCADE.

A LA FIN DU FESTIVAL, LA PAUVRE MAIN QUI DESSINE EST FOUTUE!

TRANSLATION - JEAN-PIERRE MERCIER

Angoulême, first page of a fully drawn account of the Angoulême festival, in the French daily Libération, Paris, France.

Second page of a fully drawn account of the Angoulême festival, in the French daily Libération, Paris, France.

"....If you could manage it, landing knees-first on some-one's kidneys was the most brutal."
R. CRUMB '86

...JUST MARRIED!

Season's Greetings!
R. CRUMB '86

Illustration for a story. Publisher unknown.

Just Married, card, Julian Schiller & Diane Callum.

Season's Greetings, card made for the McNamara family

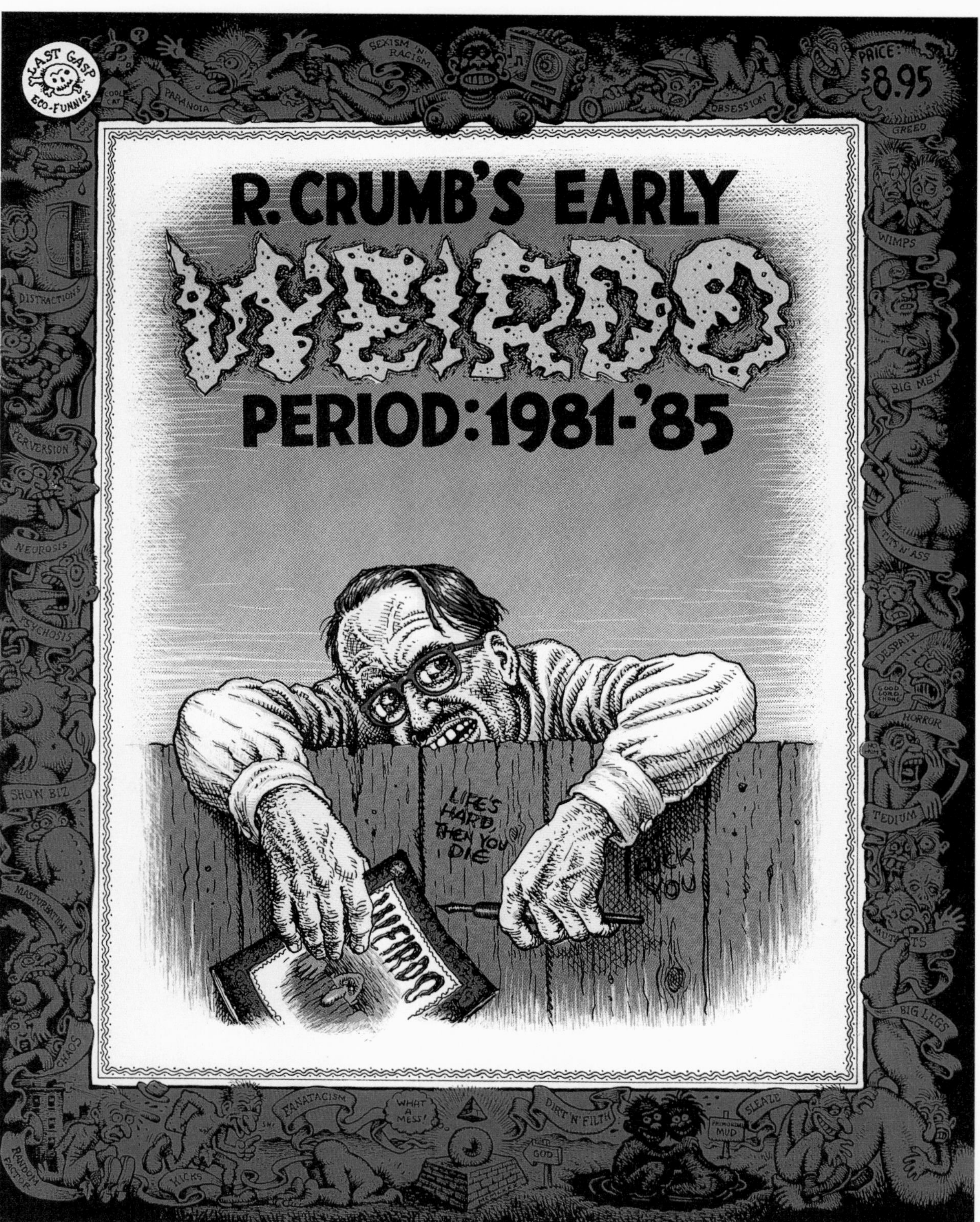

R. Crumb's Early Weirdo period: 1981-'85, book cover, Last Gasp Eco-Funnies, Berkeley, Ca.

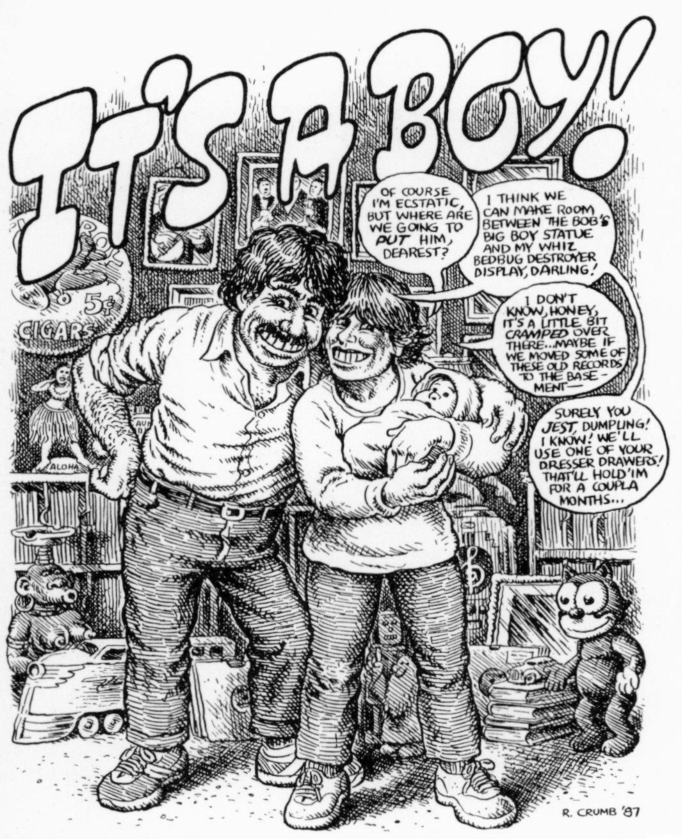
IT'S A BOY!
OF COURSE I'M ECSTATIC, BUT WHERE ARE WE GOING TO PUT HIM, DEAREST?
I THINK WE CAN MAKE ROOM BETWEEN THE BOB'S BIG BOY STATUE AND MY WHIZ BEDBUG DESTROYER DISPLAY, DARLING!
I DON'T KNOW, HONEY, IT'S A LITTLE BIT CRAMPED OVER THERE...MAYBE IF WE MOVED SOME OF THESE OLD RECORDS TO THE BASE-MENT—
SURELY YOU JEST, DUMPLING! I KNOW! WE'LL USE ONE OF YOUR DRESSER DRAWERS! THAT'LL HOLD 'IM FOR A COUPLA MONTHS...
CIGARS
5¢
ALOHA
R. CRUMB '87

Françoise
by R. CRUMB
AUGUST '87

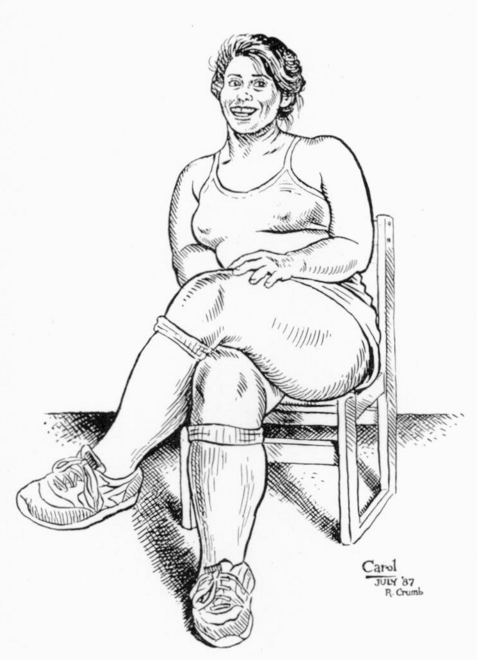
Carol
JULY '87
R. Crumb

LAISSEZ GOODSTUFF ROULÉ
TOUT le TEMPS, PARDNER
WINTERS, CALIFORNIA
R. CRUMB '87

It's a Boy!,
birth announcement card.

Françoise.

R. Crumb Bares All, cover
of The Comics Journal,
number 121, with interview.
Fantagraphics Books,
Seattle.

Portrait of Carol Engberg,
oil painting.

Carol.

Laissez Goodstuff Roulé,
drawing for Goodstuff,
Winters, Ca.

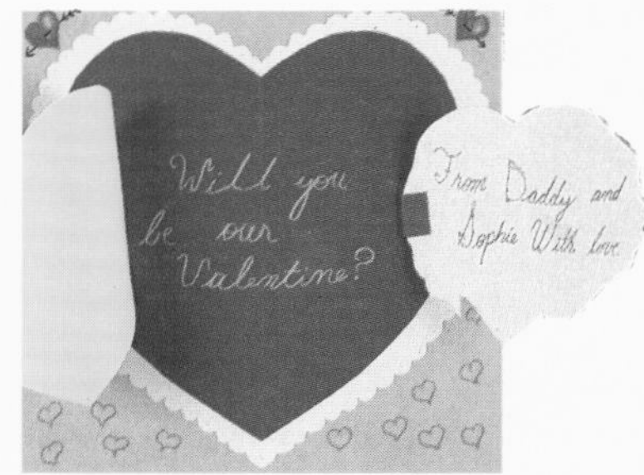

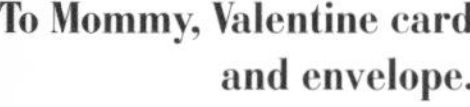

To Mommy, Valentine card
and envelope.

DR. JULIAN G. SCHILLER
CHIROPRACTOR

Leah
BY R. CRUMB
N.Y.C., OCT., '87
(LOVE & XXX!!)
DOES PHONE SEX FOR A LIVING.
GIANT JEWISH GIRL FROM THE BRONX.

ROBERT CRUMB & ALINE KOMINSKY-CRUMB
P.O. BOX 533, WINTERS, CALIFORNIA 95694
PHONE: 916·795·4379

TO MARK J. COHEN

YES, I'M BITTER... MAYBE I NEED THERAPY... IS THIS WORTH 25 BUCKS, YOU *JERK*?? JEEZIS, ANOTHER PUSHY JEW... DONT WORRY, I'M NOT ANTI-SEMITIC... I HATE ALL RACES EQUALLY... SPEAKING OF PUSHY JEWS, NOW YOU TAKE MY WIFE... I MEAN, IF ANYBODY HAS A RIGHT TO BE ANTI-SEMITIC, IT'S ME... I'VE HAD TWO JEWISH WIVES AWREADY... IT'S A WONDER I'M STILL WALKIN' AROUND... IT'S REALLY A WONDER I CAN STILL GET IT UP... WELL, SOMETIMES... SORTA... SERIOUSLY, THOUGH... AS MY MOTHER-IN-LAW ONCE SAID, "NO, BUT HE LOVES THE JEWS..." ALOT OF PEOPLE THINK I'M JEWISH... ANYBODY WHO HATES HIMSELF THAT MUCH *MUST* BE JEWISH... WHY DO THESE JEWISH WOMEN ZERO IN ON ME? THEY LIKE AHTISTS OR SOMETHING, I DUNNO... MY WIFE'S VERY OFFENDED THAT YOU DON'T WANT HER TO DO A SELF-PORTRAIT... SHE'S A CAHTOONIST TOO, Y'KNOW... JUST AS GOOD AS ME WHEN IT COMES DOWN TO IT... FUNNIER, ACTUALLY... SHE'S A GREAT JEWISH STORY TELLER... BUT NO, I'VE GOT THE NAME... IT'S *ME* THEY WANT... IT'S ME THEY PESTER... HEY, IT'S THE PRICE OF FAME,... YEAH SURE, BUT WHERE'S MY BLOW JOB IN THE ELEVATOR, THE REST ROOM WITH THE BEAUTIFUL WAITRESS... NO-O-O... I DONT GET *THAT* PART... ONLY THE AGGRAVATION... BUT WHY AM I TELLING *YOU* ALL THIS?? I DON'T EVEN *KNOW* YOU AND I'VE GOT A MILLION OTHER LETTERS PILED UP HERE FULL OF DEMANDS... MOST OF THEM DONT CONTAIN CHECKS, HOWEVER... A CHEAP JEW TRICK BUT IT WORKS ON ME... BUT I LOVE THE JEWS SO DONT GET UPSET... DONT GET NERVOUS... I'LL SAY GOOD-BYE NOW...

MARCH '87

Fried Brains, commissioned by a guy for his filmscript.

Leah, a giant Jewish girl from the Bronx who does phone sex for a living.

Is This a Match Made in Heaven or What?!?, wedding announcement of Craig and Julie McNamara.

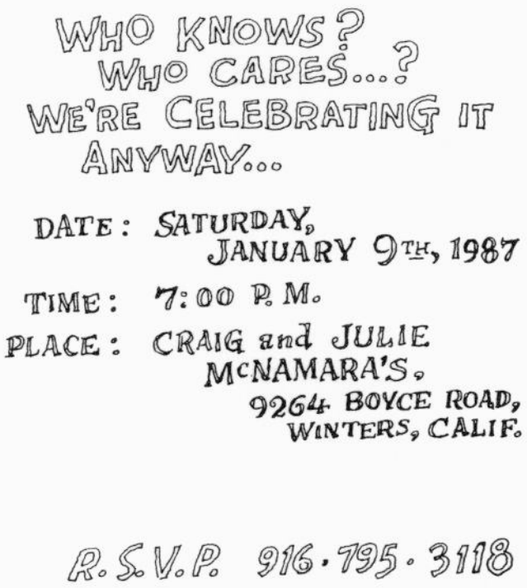

Who Knows? Who Cares? We're Celebrating it Anyway, wedding announcement (inside) of Craig and Julie McNamara.

Have Yourself an Expressionistic Little Christmas, Christmas card from the Crumb family.

Mr. Natural Sez: Chiropractic... Naturally!, Dr. Julian G. Schiller, chiropractor. Probably an advertisement.

Self-portrait, to Mark J. Cohen.

Unpublished illustration.

IS THIS A MATCH MADE IN HEAVEN OR WHAT?!?

WHO KNOWS? WHO CARES...? WE'RE CELEBRATING IT ANYWAY...

DATE: SATURDAY, JANUARY 9TH, 1987

TIME: 7:00 P.M.

PLACE: CRAIG and JULIE McNAMARA'S, 9264 BOYCE ROAD, WINTERS, CALIF.

R.S.V.P. 916·795·3118

"...AND SO ONCE AGAIN THE SUN SHINED IN THE VALLEY!"

DON'T SAY I DIDN'T WARN YOU!!

POLITICIAN

SCIENTIST

THE GOV.

CALIFORNIA SUPERCOLLIDER BANDWAGON

OUR TAX DOLLARS

— R. CRUMB '88

Lauren
by R. CRUMB
Sept., 1988

Michelle
by R. CRUMB
Sept., '88

Carol
Vinson
by R. CRUMB
AUGUST '88

ALINE TURNS 40
NO-O-O-O
R. CRUMB, AGE 45.
...AND SHE WANTS A BIG WILD PARTY!
SO WE'RE GOING TO "GET IT ON" AT JULIE & CRAIG McNAMARA'S,
SATURDAY, SEPT. 3RD, 1988, 8:00 P.M. — R.S.V.P. 916·795·3118

Lauren.

Michelle.

Carol Vinson.

Elisa.

Carol Engberg.

Carol Vinson.

The Complete Crumb Comics, volume 3: Commercial Artist. This cover design was rejected by publisher Fantagraphics.

Aline Turns 40, invitation from the McNamara family.

DON'T TRY TO HATCH IT UP TOO MUCH!
Carol Engberg
-R. CRUMB
AUGUST 1988

LET'S BUILD A

PLAYGROUND

IN CITY PARK FOR THE CHILDREN OF **WINTERS!**

WE HAVE A GREAT IDEA TO BUILD A PLAYGROUND THAT IS:

- ★ FUN
- ★ SAFE
- ★ STIMULATING FOR KIDS OF ALL AGES
- ★ A SHADY AND PLEASANT PLACE FOR PARENTS
- ★ A PROJECT THAT WILL PROMOTE COMMUNITY SPIRIT

IF YOU'D LIKE TO BE A PART OF MAKING THIS HAPPEN, COME TO A

TOWN MEETING

TUESDAY, NOVEMBER 15th, 1988, 7:30 P.M.
WINTERS COMMUNITY CENTER

ENTHUSIASTICALLY SUPPORTED BY:

JULIE & CRAIG McNAMARA
NIKI HARRIS
BOBBIE GREENWOOD
LINDA MARIANI
MARY LOU LINVIL
ALLAN PEDERSON
ALINE & ROBERT CRUMB
MONICA CRANSTON
LESLIE & PETER HANSEN
SARAH JEWEL
DR. STEPHEN NEWMAN, M.D.
DIANE & JEFF BEATON
DEBBIE HEMENWAY

Flyer: 20th Anniversary Zap Comics, Last Gasp, San Francisco.

Birth announcement card.

Have a Merry Christmas, Christmas card for the McNamara family.

Your Mother Would Want You to Eat Like This!, drawing for Goodstuff, Winters, Ca.

Flyer: Let's Build a Playground.

Anything For Money, illustration for a screenplay by Terry Zwigoff & R. Crumb.

OOH AHH
SHE'S A SAVAGE FORCE OF NATURE....
GRAAK
R. CRUMB
R. CRUMB '88

She's a Savage Force of Nature, cover drawing for Screw magazine, number 1024.

Sassy, illustration for a film-script by Terry Zwigoff & R. Crumb.

Sassy, title page illustration for a film-script by Terry Zwigoff & R. Crumb.

Alice
AUGUST '89
R. CRUMB

Julia
by
R. CRUMB '89
6'2" IRISH-ITALIAN,
RED HAIR, GREW UP IN
GREENWICH VILLAGE, WHERE
MOTHER OWNS A BAR

Alice
R. CRUMB
AUGUST 1989

Carol Vinson
–R. CRUMB '89

New York City, May, 1989...
LESLIE, BEING SOMEWHAT INEBRIATED, STUMBLES AND FALLS DOWN IN THE STREET...
A CAR THEN RUNS OVER HER CALF—FRONT AND REAR WHEELS BOTH! THE DRIVER DOESN'T STOP, BUT CONTINUES ON HIS WAY. LESLIE GETS UP AND WALKS AWAY WITH ONLY MINOR BRUISES AND TREAD IMPRINTS ON HER JUMPSUIT!!!
HER THOUGHT AT THAT MOMENT
HMM! THAT CAR'S NOT VERY HEAVY...
FOR LESLIE WITH REVERENCE— R. CRUMB '89

Portrait of Alice.

Julia, 6'2" Irish-Italian, red hair, grew up in Greenwich Village where her mother owns a bar.

Portrait of Alice.

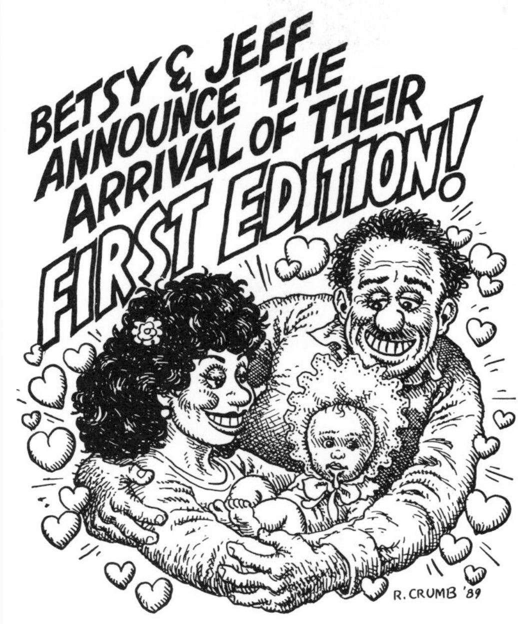

Betsy & Jeff Announce the Arrival of Their First Edition, cover illustration for a birth announcement card, Jeffry & Betsy Weinberg.

We Welcome With Joy Molly Courtney, inside birth announcement card, Jeffry & Betsy Weinberg.

"THE JOHNNY APPLESEED OF PLAYGROUNDS,"
ROBERT LEATHERS
IS COMING TO WINTERS!
... & YOU'RE INVITED TO COME & MEET HIM.

FRIDAY, FEB. 24th 7:30 P.M. at the WINTERS COMMUNITY CENTER

FOR MORE INFORMATION CALL: JULIE McNAMARA 795-3118 OR: PEG ASHMORE 795-4388

WE'LL PROVIDE: FUN & FOOD

PLEASE BRING: IDEAS ? QUESTIONS ? ? ? ? ENTHUSIASM

SEE THE PLAYGROUND DESIGNED BY THE CHILDREN OF WINTERS & ROBERT LEATHERS!
WE CAN BUILD IT TOGETHER!
SPONSORED BY THE CITY PARK PLAYGROUND COMMITTEE

Go and Fuck Thyself, postcard, Glenn Bray, Sylmar, Ca.

The Johnny Appleseed of Playgrounds, poster.

Portrait of Leslie.

Portrait of Carol Vinson, slightly reworked print of February 1990.

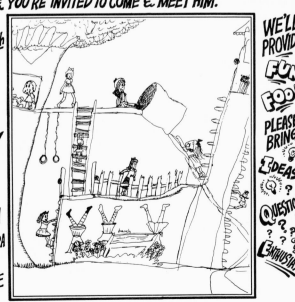

ANTI-PORN: THE DEATH OF OPPRESSION

Toilets That Kill / Enema of the People / Sex-Crazed Stewardesses

SCREW

$2.00 | **THE SEX REVIEW** | **NUMBER 1,040**

Cover: ROBERT CRUMB

WARNING: Sexual material of an adult nature. This literature is not intended for minors and under no circumstances are they to view it, possess it, or place orders for merchandise offered herein.

The Pressure's On..., cover of Screw magazine, number 1040.

True Life Romances, cover drawing for Screw magazine, number 1076.

Cover drawing for Screw magazine, number 1059.

HE YEARNED FOR A LIFE OF QUIET STUDY, HIGH ABOVE THIS VAIL OF TRIBULATION AND TEARS...
AH HMM
R. CRUMB '89

SO??
R. CRUMB '89

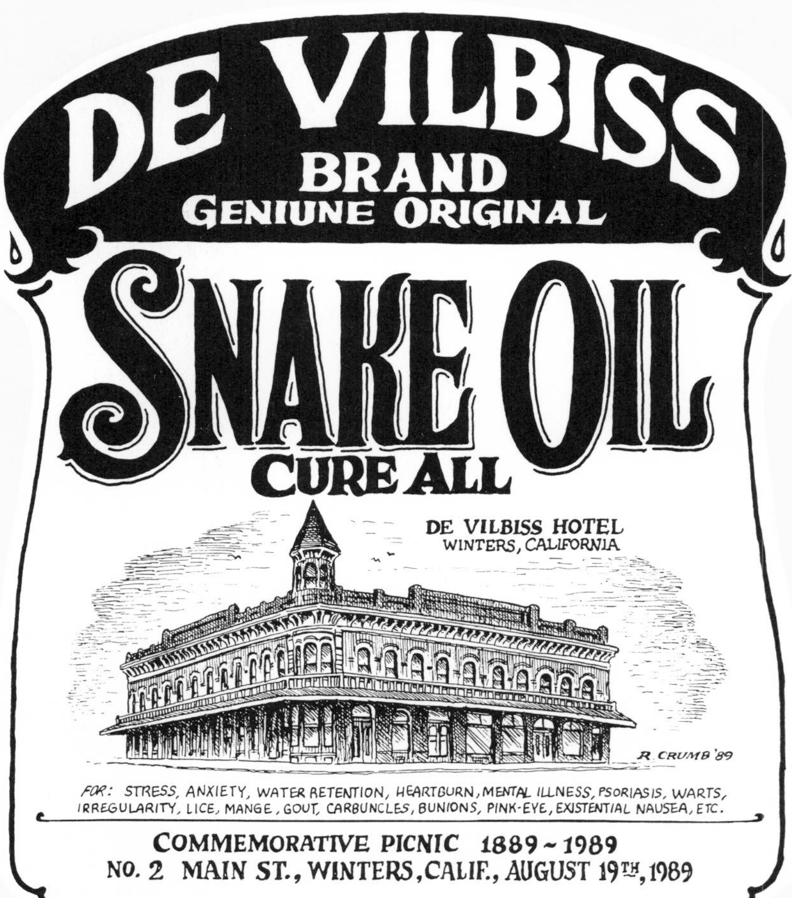
DE VILBISS
BRAND
GENIUNE ORIGINAL
SNAKE OIL
CURE ALL
DE VILBISS HOTEL
WINTERS, CALIFORNIA
R. CRUMB '89
FOR: STRESS, ANXIETY, WATER RETENTION, HEARTBURN, MENTAL ILLNESS, PSORIASIS, WARTS, IRREGULARITY, LICE, MANGE, GOUT, CARBUNCLES, BUNIONS, PINK-EYE, EXISTENTIAL NAUSEA, ETC.
COMMEMORATIVE PICNIC 1889 ~ 1989
NO. 2 MAIN ST., WINTERS, CALIF., AUGUST 19TH, 1989

Drawing for Goodstuff, Winters, Ca.

CHERRY COLA
R. CRUMB '89
GOODSTUFF
DOWNHILL BOTH WAYS GUARANTEED
306 RAILROAD AVE.
WINTERS, CALIFORNIA
ON THE SUNSET SIDE OF THE GREAT SACRAMENTO VALLEY

Calendar for bookstore Carlson & Turner

So??, self-portrait for Fantagraphics.

De Vilbiss Snake Oil, promotional label for fake old time medicine bottles, sold at Commemorative Picnic, Winters, Ca.

Emile Vacher.

HAPPY 9th BIRTHDAY SOPHIE!
AW! MY LITTLE GIRL IS GROWING UP!
NO, SHE'LL ALWAYS BE OUR BABY!
SMOOCH
SMORP

NO KISSING!
YUK!!
MUSHY STUFF!
OY!
From those two Wacky Zany Parental Units That Love You So Much!!

CAROLINE'S
PROGRAM PAGES 19 & 22
MAY 1990
LAUGHTRACK
...BUT SERIOUSLY, AM I SHAKING? IS IT OBVIOUS?? IF ONLY I COULD REMEMBER MY MATERIAL... I—I NEVER COULD TELL A JOKE...IZZAT OKAY? THANK YOU... YOU'RE A VERY CIVILIZED AUDIENCE...I HATE IT WHEN I HAVE TO CALL FOR SECURITY... YEAH,SO,UH, AWRIGHT... LOVE YA... HAVE A GOOD ONE,AN' ....LIKE THAT...
R. CRUMB '90
SIXTIES-ISH
FEATURING: R. CRUMB & MR. NATURAL'S SHARP COMEBACKS
AND DR. TIMOTHY LEARY'S RETURN TRIP

Happy 9th Birthday Sophie!, cover and inside drawing of birthday card.

Vulture Goddess Statue, photograph.

Cover of Caroline's Laugh Track magazine, J. Abram Publishing.

Hell Hound on My Trail, silk-screen print of Robert Johnson.

OVER 40, SO WHAT!
WINTERS, CALIFORNIA

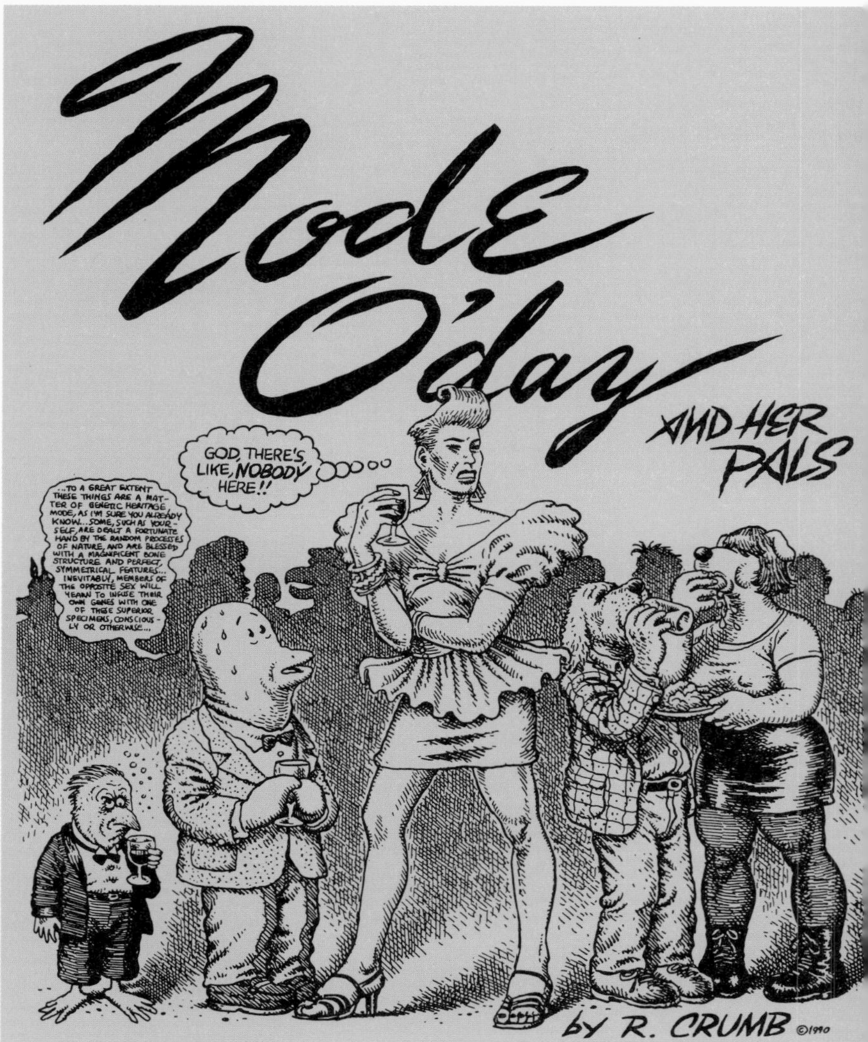

Nancy, the nose was reworked in July 1993.

Illustration for Winters Bike Shop.

Over 40, So What!, advertisement for Goodstuff, Winters, Ca.

Bikini Battle 3D, illustration.

Mode O'day and Her Pals, used for a French edition.

Mitchell Brothers, 'cocktail napkin' for the Mitchell Brothers Porn Theatre, San Francisco.

We Wish You a Merry Christmas!
R. Crumb 1990

From Julie, Craig, Graham and Sean

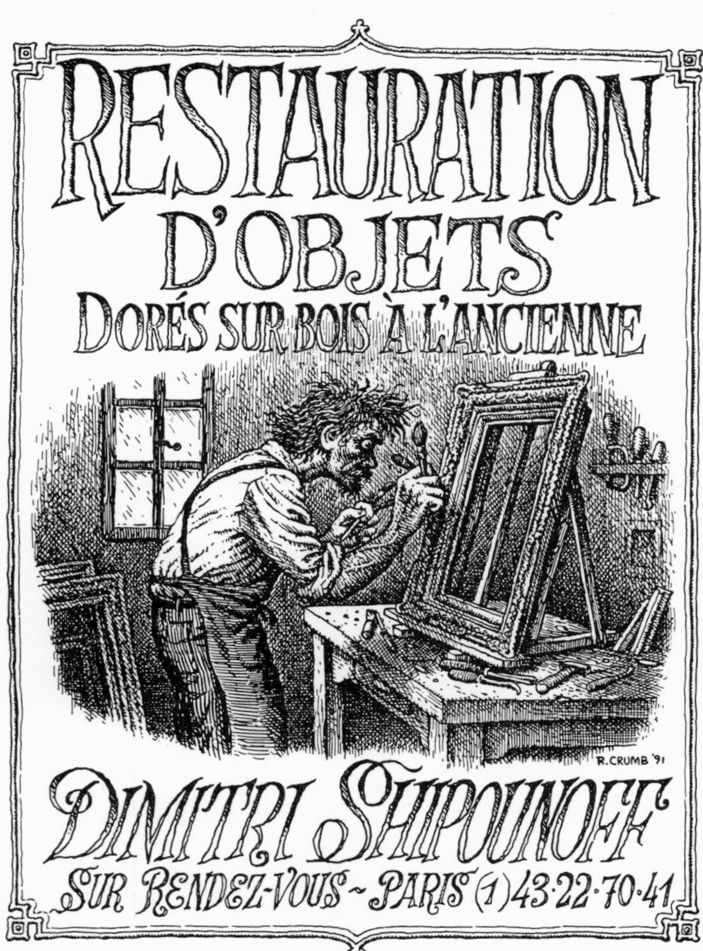
RESTAURATION
D'OBJETS
DORÉS SUR BOIS À L'ANCIENNE
R. CRUMB '91
DIMITRI SHIPOUNOFF
SUR RENDEZ-VOUS ~ PARIS (1) 43·22·70·41

You're just too much and oh so very very...
to ever be in Webster's Dictionary...
And so I'm whispering a love song from the birds,
to tell you that you're marvelous,
too marvelous for words!

The Reardon Children
and their families
invite you to join in
the celebration of
Marge & Jim's
50th Wedding
Anniversary
at 4:00 P.M.,
Saturday, June 16th, 1990
at Chelsea Commons
(A.K.A. Café James Jr.)
463 West 24th Street,
New York, N.Y.
R.S.V.P.
203-865-0180
(Sheila)

U.S.M.C.
R. CRUMB

1990

We Wish You
a Merry Christmas,
Christmas card from
the McNamara family.

Restaurant
Le Micocoulier,
calling card.
1991

RESTAURANT
le Micocoulier
CUISINE DU MONDE ENTIER
3 PL. J. ASTRUC, 30610 SAUVE Tel: 66·77·57·61

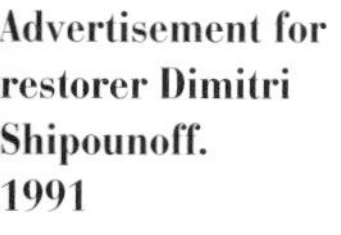

Advertisement for
restorer Dimitri
Shipounoff.
1991

Invitation card to
celebrate the 50th
wedding anniversary of
Mr. and Mrs. Reardon,
issued by Julie Reardon
McNamara.

Portrait of H.C. Wester-
mann, illustration for
The New Yorker,
April 8, 1991.

Marilyn Montreuil,
illustration/advertisement
for the musical comedy
Marilyn Montreuil by
J. Savary & D. Tell.
1991

OIL 'N' BLOOD

War News

ILLUSTRATED AND UNCENSORED

R. CRUMB 1991

Invitation for an exhibition, Arcade.

Made on request in exchange for old records.

War News, headline of War News, volume 1, number 1, a Gulf War newspaper. Published by Warren Hinckle.

Le Monde Selon Crumb, promotion poster for C.N.B.D.I. in Angoulême, France.

LA FERME DE COUTACH, SAUVE

WOODY GUTHRIE

ALAN DERSHOWITZ
BY R. CRUMB '92

Le Ferme de Coutach, Sauve. Unpublished.

Bloody Incompetent French, birthday drawing for Nick.

Woodie Guthrie, illustration for The New Yorker.

Alan Dershowitz, illustration for The New Yorker.

Self-portrait, cover design for Hulp Comics. Project of Last Gasp, San Francisco. Unpublished.

INNUENDO

SEPT. 1993

R. CRUMB '93

George Jones

DEAR GOD, WHY WON'T THEY LISTEN TO ME!?!

R. CRUMB '93

Cover of Innuendo, September 1993.

George Jones, illustration for The New Yorker.

Self-portrait for The Comics Journal, Seattle.

The Rise and Fall of Third Leg, cover of a book by Jon Longhi, Manic D Press, San Francisco.

Espoir Perdu, portrait.

Erica.

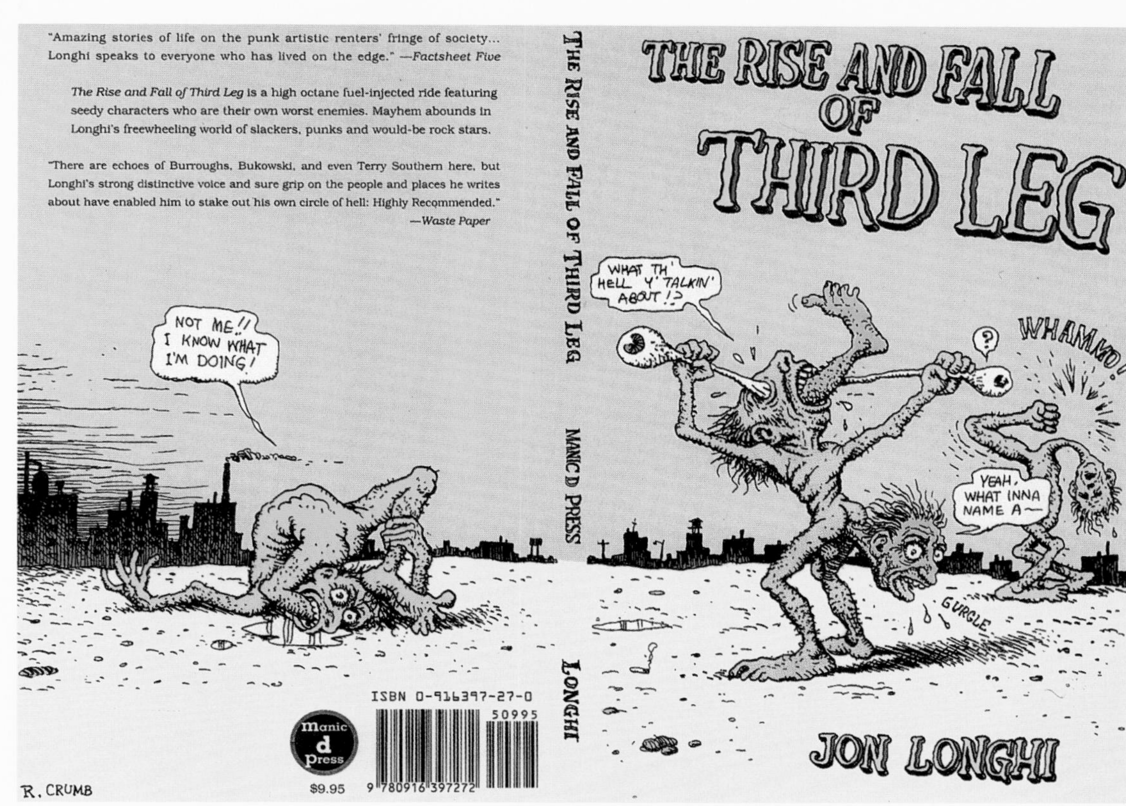

R. CRUMB'S RECURRING DREAM OF FLYING...

Have a Good'n!

HUH HUH... HUH HUH HUH

WHAT-EVER!

SO HOW 'BOUT THOSE PHOENICIANS!

XIII

WE GOT A GOOD LITTLE IRONY GOIN' HERE!

WE LIVE FOR THE PRETTY THINGS...

Joyeux Noël

from Les Crumb

Robert, Aline, Sophie, Erica, and Jesse

R. Crumb's Recurring Dream of Flying..., comic for Yugoslavian comic artist's Dream Book. Not yet published.

Have a Good 'n! Joyeux Noël, Christmas card from the Crumb family.

Illustration for a story written by David Mairowitz (the writer of Kafka for Beginners), about a midget wrestler who wrestles with girls in a small village in the south of France. Unpublished.

—R. CRUMB '94

Chuck You Farley! - Fark You Chuckley!, drawn at the request of a comic fan's wife.

THERE GOES OUR LITTLE GIRL!

Devil Girl Choco-Bar, T-shirt print. Published by Kitchen Sink Press, Northampton, Mass.

R. Crumb's Devil Girl Choco-Bar, top, side and bottom of box. Kitchen Sink Press, Northampton, Mass.

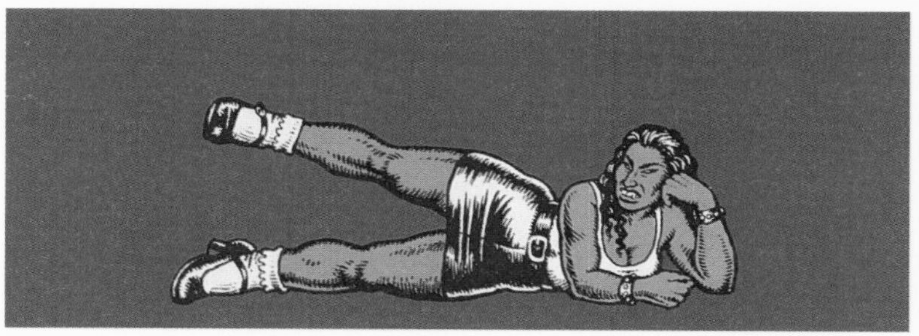

Cover of The New Yorker.

Soph, Now That You're 13 You're Officially a Teen-Ager, birthday card.

REGARDONS-LES EN FACE,
GARDONS-LES EN SURFACE
R. CRUMB '94
LE GARD DIT :
NON À L'ENFOUISSEMENT DES DÉCHETS RADIOACTIFS!

MORAND
CAJUN
BAND
R. CRUMB

R. CRUMB '94

Regardons-Les en Face, Gardons-Les en Surface, picture postcard, published by Collectif Rhodanieu Contre l'Enfouissement des Déchets Radioactifs.

Drawing for Alex Acevedo - Big Swap Meet - at his gallery in New York. It was his idea, in exchange for a 1920's Andy Gump toy. Unpublished.

Drawing for the Morand Cajun Band.

Hey Kids! Look Who's Back in Town, drawing for Hansje Joustra, managing director of Oog & Blik.

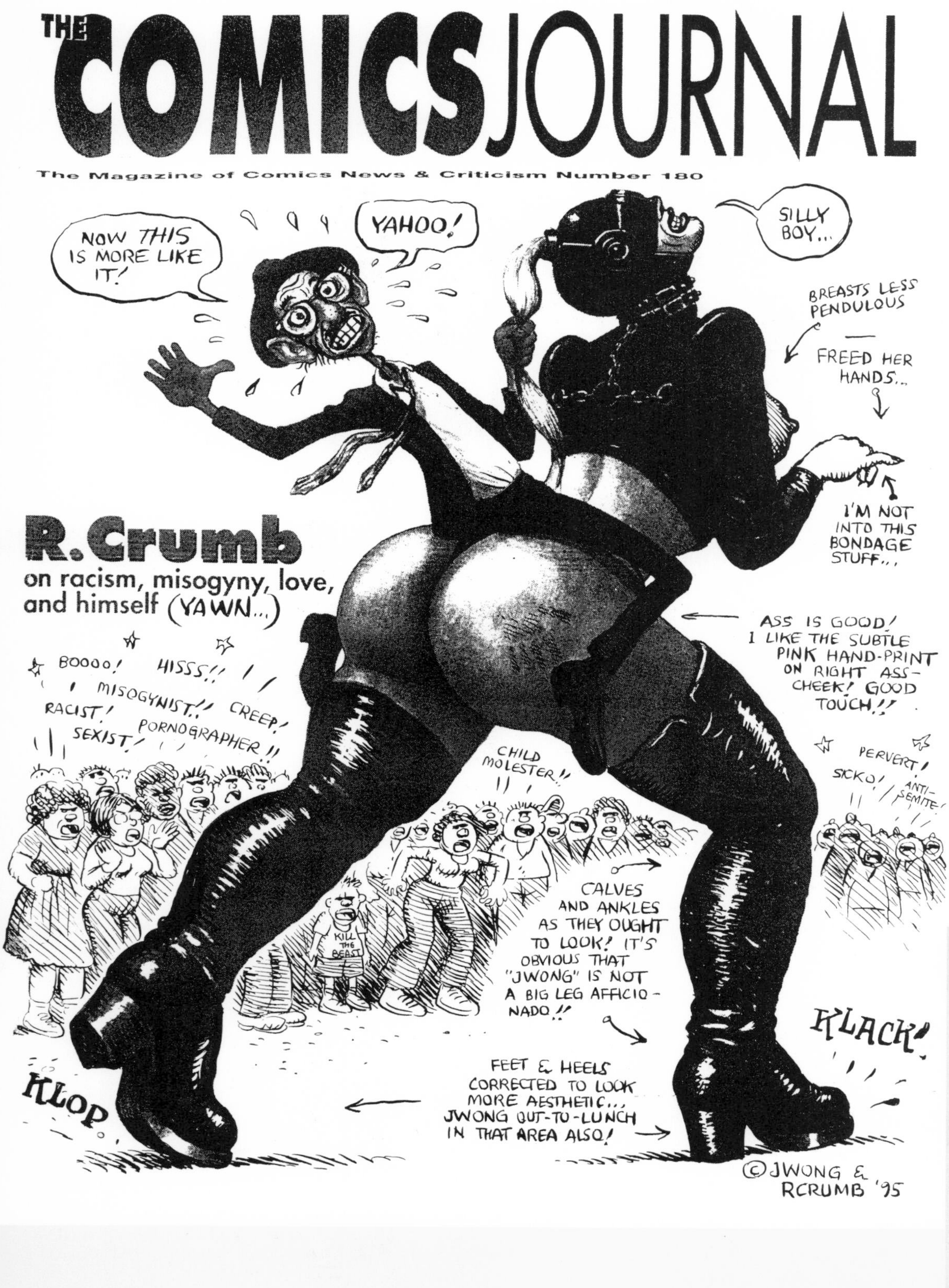

THE COMICS JOURNAL

The Magazine of Comics News & Criticism Number 180

NOW THIS IS MORE LIKE IT!

YAHOO!

SILLY BOY...

BREASTS LESS PENDULOUS

FREED HER HANDS...

I'M NOT INTO THIS BONDAGE STUFF...

R. Crumb
on racism, misogyny, love, and himself (YAWN...)

ASS IS GOOD! I LIKE THE SUBTLE PINK HAND-PRINT ON RIGHT ASS-CHEEK! GOOD TOUCH!!

BOOOO! HISSS!! MISOGYNIST!! CREEP! RACIST! PORNOGRAPHER!! SEXIST!

CHILD MOLESTER!!

PERVERT! SICKO! ANTI-SEMITE!

KILL THE BEAST

CALVES AND ANKLES AS THEY OUGHT TO LOOK! IT'S OBVIOUS THAT "JWONG" IS NOT A BIG LEG AFFICIO-NADO!!

KLACK!

KLOP

FEET & HEELS CORRECTED TO LOOK MORE AESTHETIC... JWONG OUT-TO-LUNCH IN THAT AREA ALSO!

©JWONG & RCRUMB '95

Reworked cover of The Comics Journal, number 180.

Portrait of R. Crumb by J. Wong on cover of The Comics Journal, number 180, Fantagraphics Books, Seattle.

R. Crumb's First Impression of Finland, for Kemi, a Finnish newspaper.

Vic Pratt, a young aspiring cartoonist from England, sent a drawing of himself to R. Crumb and asked him to draw himself, while shaking hands with him.

The Trick Is to Keep in Shape, birthday card for Sharon.

Mr. Natural and His Pal R. Crumb. Drawn at the request of a comic art collector in exchange for a rare record which Crumb stated in Self-Loathing Comics he was looking for (Having Lots of Fun, by Jules Herbuveaux, Palmer House, 1927).

SIGNING BOOKPLATES

THIS IS A PUNISHMENT!

UN-SIGNED

SIGNED

R. CRUMB '95

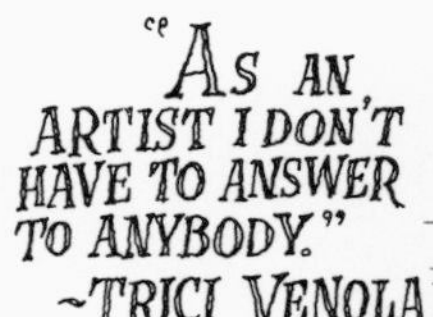

Signing Bookplates, ex libris for Carload O' Comics, Kitchen Sink Press, Northampton, Mass.

Trici Venola.

R. CRUMB
1995
THE CHEAP SUIT SERENADERS
ROBERT ARMSTRONG, R. CRUMB, ALLAN DODGE; DIXON, CALIFORNIA, 1973

The Cheap Suit Serenaders, copied from an old photograph, requested by Al Dodge in exchange for some old 78 rpm records.

Françoise.

Annie, Sauve, France.

Drawing for a brochure to promote a friend's vacation spots, Sauve, France.

The Music Never Stopped®

ROOTS of the GRATEFUL DEAD®

with OBRAY RAMSEY · MERLE HAGGARD · DIXIE CUPS · CANNON'S JUG STOMPERS · BOB DYLAN
CHUCK BERRY · MARTY ROBBINS · CHARLEY PATTON · HOWLING WOLF · BOBBY BLUE BLAND
HENRY THOMAS · BUDDY HOLLY · BONNIE DOBSON · WOODY GUTHRIE · JOSEPH SPENCE · JIMMIE REED
REV. GARY DAVIS

R. CRUMB '95

GÉRARD DÔLE
10 RUE DE BUCI 75006 PARIS FRANCE
TEL: (1)43 26 59 81 FAX: (1)43 25 97 72

The Music Never Stopped, Roots of the Grateful Dead, cd cover and advertisement.

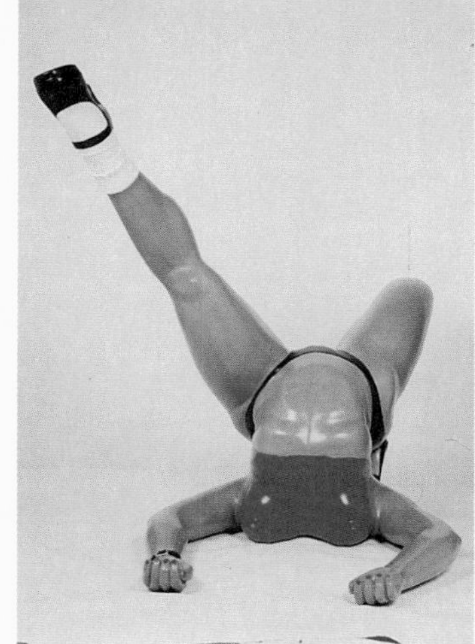

Devil Girl, statue. Photographs.

Calling card for Gérard Dôle.

Letter-head for Jazztrash South (Anthony Baldwin).

Réserve du Micocoulier
Restaurant à Sauve

ALC. 13.5% VOL. 750 ML.

COSTIÈRES DE NIMES
APPELLATION COSTIÈRES DE NIMES CONTRÔLÉE
MIS EN BOUTEILLE AU DOMAINE

DOMAINE DE RAPATEL
C. EYRAUD, PROPRIETAIRE
RÉCOLTANTE À CAISSARGUES
30132 FRANCE

Singin' in the Bathtub, illustration originally done in 1987 as a promo for a bathroom supply warehouse in exchange for bathroom fixtures. Metal sign. Reworked in 1996 for Kitchen Sink Press, Northampton, Mass.

Réserve du Micocoulier, detail and complete wine label for restaurant Micocoulier, Sauve, France.

Swimming Pool, drawing for a brochure to promote a friend's vacation spots, Sauve, France.

Merle Haggard, illustration for The New Yorker.

Festival de Trompette, advertisement, Sauve, France.

~A VOICE OF MY OWN~

A Voice of My Own, requested by Crumb's sister Carol (fourth from right). Crumb used photographs of other women and put costumes on them according to his sister's instructions. The woman are all prominent authors from different eras and of different nationalities.

Big Sport, record label. 1997

Amos Easton Known as Bumble Bee Slim, illustration for an article on Bumble Bee Slim by Jerry Zolten, in exchange for old 78 rpm records. 1997

Portret of Bessie Smith and Clarence Williams, drawn in exchange for old 78 rpm records. 1997

Low Life, record label for Tony Boldwin.

Calling card for Het Raadsel (Hansje Joustra). 1997

Calling card for Oog & Blik (Hansje Joustra). 1997

BIG SPORT
ELECTRIC RECORDS
So Sweet
Jimmie Noone & his Apex Club Orchestra
C-59028
R. CRUMB '97
AMOS EASTON
KNOWN AS
"BUMBLE BEE SLIM"
Bessie Smith and Clarence Williams recording
"Need A Little Sugar In My Bowl"
for Columbia Records
New York, Feb., 1931
R. CRUMB '97

R. CRUMB
and his
Li'l Ol'
Banjo
Dec, '98

FLASHBACKS
AND
PREMONITIONS
STORIES BY
JON LONGHI

IT'S O.K., I WON'T LET KENNETH STARR GET YOU!
HOLD ME, ALINE!

R. Crumb and His Li'l Ol' Banjo, drawing for a silk-screen print.

Cover of Flashbacks and Premonitions, Stories by Jon Longhi, Manic D.Press, San Francisco.

Hold Me, Aline!, illustration for The New Yorker, September 28.

How Sweet It Is! For a Privileged Few..., comic for The New Yorker, September 28.

HAPPY 53RD BIRTHDAY TO THE OTHER HUSBAND!

DON'T YOU THINK THESE NEW PANTS LOOK SEXY ON ME, NOW THAT I'M IN BETTER SHAPE THAN I'VE BEEN IN YEARS?! I WEIGH 133 POUNDS NOW, WHICH IS MY PERFECT WEIGHT! I HAVE NO DESIRE TO LOSE ANY MORE—I'M A LOT LESS NEUROTIC THAN I USED TO BE—I USED TO THINK I HAD TO BE BONE THIN—EAT THAT LEFT OVER CHICKEN CURRY TONIGHT, OTHERWISE IT'LL GO BAD—IF SOPHIE CALLS TELL HER I'LL PICK HER UP—I'VE WORKED OUT THE BEST EXERCISE PROGRAM I EVER HAD—I LOOK GREAT FOR MY AGE, RIGHT?!?

OH, YES...

UH, WELL—

OKAY...

I—

OH ABSOLUTELY—I—

"HIP HUGGAS"

MAY YOU HAVE MANY MORE!!

Happy 53rd Birthday to The Other Husband! May You Have Many More!! Double birthday card drawn for Christian Coudurès, Sauve.

Portrait of Michael and Dieter, drawn in exchange for old 78 rpm records.

Big Healthy Girl Enjoys Deep Penetration From The Rear.

Portrait of Tina Lockwood for an art show about women body builders, New York.

Save The Wolves, illustration.

MONICA DELIVERS THE PIZZA...
SO, LISTEN, "SONNY", I-UH-UH.....
OH DEAR JEEZUZ...
THAT BILL'S A LUCKY GUY! — R. CRUMB, '98

Monica Delivers The Pizza..., illustration for Rolling Stone, New York.

Amour, Disques et Collection, comic drawn in exchange for old 78 rpm records.

HUNTING FOR OLD RECORDS

A TRUE STORY

by R. CRUMB 1999

THE YEAR WAS 1960. THE AUTHOR WAS IN HIS LATE TEENS, LIVING WITH HIS PARENTS IN DOVER, DELAWARE.

I LOVE THIS OLD MUSIC! I MUST FIND MORE OLD BLUES AND JAZZ RECORDS FROM THE 'TWENTIES!

AFTER A FRUITLESS DAY OF KNOCKING ON DOORS IN THE BLACK SECTION, I WAS ABOUT TO CALL IT QUITS...

HAVEN'T SEEN A SINGLE WORTHWHILE RECORD TODAY...I'LL TRY ONE MORE HOUSE...

UHH...HM, WHY YES, IN FACT I DO HAVE SOME OLD RECORDS... HOW MUCH DO YOU PAY?

I CAN PAY TEN CENTS. MAYBE A QUARTER FOR A REALLY GOOD ONE...

THAT'S NOT MUCH... BUT I S'POSE YOU CAN HAVE A LOOK... YOU MAY COME IN...

...A BUNCH OF SWING BANDS FROM THE 'THIRTIES...NO INTEREST TO ME... BUT WHAT'S THIS!?! "GOOFUS" AND "HAPPY" BY SLIM LAMAR'S SOUTHERNERS ON THE LATE 'TWENTIES VICTOR SCROLL LABEL!!

WELL, I—UH—I ONLY FOUND ONE THAT I'M INTERESTED IN...THIS ONE HERE...

HOW MUCH IS IT WORTH TO YOU?

WOULD YOU TAKE TEN CENTS FOR IT?

OH NO, DEFINITELY NOT! NOSSIR!

WELL, THEN, UM... HOW 'BOUT TWENTY-FIVE CENTS?

I KNOW THAT RECORD IS WORTH MORE'N 25 CENTS! YOU THINK I WAS BORN YESTERDAY??

WULL, I JUST CAN'T PAY ANYMORE THAN THAT... I DON'T HAVE MUCH MONEY,* AND I—

I'M NOT GONNA SELL YOU THAT RECORD FOR NO 25 CENTS, YOU MAY REST ASSURED!

B-BUT—

SNATCH!

* TRUE—I HAD A HANDFUL OF CHANGE TO MY NAME! I HAD NEVER PAID MORE THAN 25 CENTS FOR A RECORD!

Portrait of Ian McCamy, friend and fellow musician.

Big Fun on The Bayou, drawing for Gérard Dôle.

Hunting For Old Records, comic.

Fifteen-Year Thing Together, celebration card for Jesse Crumb and Erica Detlefsen, Arcata, California.

YOU ARE INVITED TO A
CELEBRATION
OF JESSE CRUMB AND
ERICA DETLEFSEN'S
FIFTEEN-YEAR
THING*
TOGETHER.
(* WE DON'T KNOW WHAT ELSE TO CALL IT)
SATURDAY, SEPT. 25th, 1999
2:00 P.M.
at 3101 FICKLE HILL ROAD
ARCATA, CALIFORNIA
(RESIDENCE of DR. & MRS. JOHN KELSEY)

Beloved Music Makers Of Days Gone By

JAZZ

Jack Teagarden

Born in Vernon, Texas in 1905, Jack Teagarden took up the trombone at the age of ten. By fifeen he was playing professionally in dance orchestras and gradually made his way to New York. His bluesy trombone technique and vocal style made him welcome everywhere. In the late '20s, as the "Jazz Age" reached a fever pitch, Teagarden was playing and making records with the best white jazz musicians in New York, including Ben Pollack and his Park Central Hotel Orchestra. Some of his best recordings in this period were made with "pick-up" groups for cheap dime-store labels and issued under pseudonyms such as "Whoopee Makers" or "Dixie Jazz Band." In the later swing era Teagarden became a minor show business celebrity. He stayed active in jazz until his death in New Orleans in 1964.

BLUES

Memphis Minnie *and* Kansas Joe

Lizzie Douglas, born in Algiers, Louisiana in 1897, was raised in Memphis and learned guitar at the age of 11. She lived and worked as an itinerant musician in the Mississippi Delta before moving to Memphis in the late '20s, where she picked up the moniker "Memphis Minnie." She formed a successful musical partnership with the taciturn, brooding "Kansas Joe" McCoy (born in Raymond, Mississippi in 1905), and the pair were discovered by a Columbia Records talent scout playing in a Beale Street barbershop for dimes. From 1928 until their break-up in 1934 Minnie and Joe made several dozen records showing their exciting guitar playing and Minnie's gift for creating original and imaginative blues songs. They each continued to play professionally and record with other musicians into the 1940s, but their best performances were those they had made together in the '28 to '34 period. Joe McCoy died in 1950. Memphis Minnie lived until 1973.

COUNTRY

The North Carolina Ramblers
Charlie Poole · Posey Rorer · Roy Harvey

One of the most prolifically recorded Southern stringbands in the pioneer days of country music as a business, the North Carolina Ramblers' commercial success from 1925 to 1930 was based largely on the charming but geniune singing style of Charlie Poole. He was well-loved in the southeastern region of the United States, and his band traveled widely, performing in small-town theatres, roadhouses and school auditoriums. Poole and Rorer both consumed excessive amounts of corn liquor. Poole met his untimely death as the result of a two-week binge, commenced in celebration of an offer to perform in a Hollywood movie in 1931. He was 39 years old.

Posey Rorer was a superb traditional fiddler. His recordings of old-time fiddle tunes such as "Ragtime Annie" and "Wild Horse" are among the very best of the period.

Roy Harvey, from West Virginia, was employed as a streetcar conductor when one day Poole and Rorer happened to board his car. A conversation about music ensued and resulted in Harvey adding his guitar backup to their banjo, vocal and fiddle. His complex three-finger guitar technique set the easy-going tempo for the band's music.

Set of 3 Portraits

by R. Crumb

Beloved Music Makers Of Days Gone By, introduction plate and portraits of Jack Teagarden, Kansas Joe and Memphis Minnie, The North Carolina Ramblers, for a portfolio.

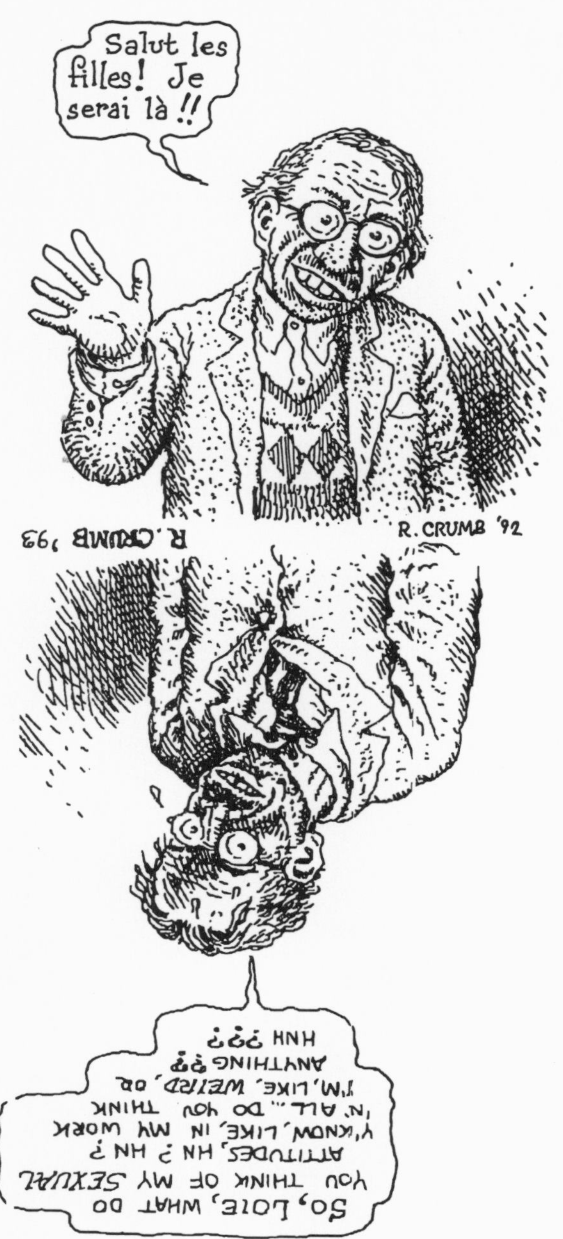
Salut les filles! Je serai là !!
R. CRUMB '92
R. CRUMB '93
SO, LOIE, WHAT DO YOU THINK OF MY SEXUAL ATTITUDES, HN? HN? Y'KNOW, LIKE, IN MY WORK 'N' ALL... DO YOU THINK I'M, LIKE, WEIRD, OR ANYTHING?? HNH???